Jenna Bess Greenberg

● **soho**
● theatre

Soho Theatre presents

Other Hands

by Laura Wade

First performed at Soho Theatre on 15 February 2006

Soho Theatre is supported by

LONDON

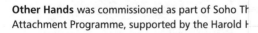

Other Hands was commissioned as part of Soho Th
Attachment Programme, supported by the Harold ʜ   dation.

Performances in the Lorenz Auditorium

Registered Charity No: 267234

Soho Theatre presents

Other Hands

by Laura Wade

Michael Gould	Greg
Richard Harrington	Steve
Anna Maxwell Martin	Hayley
Katherine Parkinson	Lydia

Director	Bijan Sheibani
Designer	Paul Burgess
Lighting Designer	Guy Kornetskzi
Sound Designer	Emma Laxton

Production Manager	Nick Ferguson
Stage Manager	Sarah Buik
Deputy Stage Manager	Helen King
Assistant Stage Manager	Geraldine Mullins

Chief Technician	Nick Blount
Chief Electrician	Christoph Wagner
Lighting Technician	Mark Watts

Scenery built and painted by   Capital Scenery Ltd

Soho Theatre would like to thank:

Emma Bennett, Campbell's Grocery Products Ltd, Microsoft for the loan of the X-Box console and Halo 2 game, Morphy Richards, James Nelson, Alexis Rose, Sadie Watts, Marissa Hoyle-Rhodes and Zoe Meads at Paul Smith, Gabriel Winn.

Paul Smith

Press Representation	Nancy Poole (020 7478 0142)
Photography	Getty Images

Soho Theatre, 21 Dean Street, London W1D 3NE
Admin: 020 7287 5060 Fax: 020 7287 5061 Box Office: 0870 429 6883
www.sohotheatre.com

Writer

Laura Wade Writer

Laura's plays include *Colder than Here* (Soho and subsequently off-Broadway at Lucille Lortel Theatre, New York for MCC); *Breathing Corpses* (Royal Court); *Young Emma* (Finborough Theatre); *16 Winters* (Bristol Old Vic); *The Wild Swans*, *Twelve Machine*, *The Last Child* (Playbox Theatre at the Dream Factory, Warwick) and *Limbo* (Crucible, Sheffield). *Breathing Corpses* earned Laura the 2005 Pearson Best Play Award and she was joint winner of the 2005 George Devine Award. In 2006 she was nominated for an Olivier Award for Outstanding Achievement.

Cast

Michael Gould Greg

Michael's theatre credits include *Pillars of the Community*, *The UN Inspector*, *The Oresteia* (National); *Cruel and Tender* (Young Vic / tour); *The Crucible* (Crucible, Sheffield); *Pericles* (Lyric Hammersmith); *King Lear*, *The Winter's Tale*, *The Maid's Tragedy* (Shakespeare's Globe); *The Sea*, *The King of Prussia* (Chichester Festival Theatre); *The Inland Sea* (Oxford Stage Company); *Phoenician Women*, *Romeo and Juliet*, *The Painter of Dishonour*, *Hamlet*, *The Dybbuk*, *A Woman Killed With Kindness*, *The Theban Trilogy*, *Twelfth Night*, *Henry IV Parts 1 and 2* (RSC); *Absurd Person Singular*, *The Tempest* (Salisbury Playhouse); *Dead Funny*, *The Tenant of Wildfell Hall* (New Victoria Theatre); *The Count of Monte Cristo* (Royal Exchange); *The Atheist's Tragedy*, *Descent* (Birmingham Rep) and *Measure for Measure*, *Twelfth Night*, *The Tempest*, *If I Were Lifted up from the Earth* (A and BC Theatre). Television credits include *Waking the Dead*, *EastEnders*, *State of Play* (BBC); *The Bill* (Thames/Talkback); *David Kelly* (Mentorn); *Green Wing* (Talkback) and *Wire In The Blood* (ITV). Film credits include *Mary Shelley's Frankenstein* (Kenneth Branagh).

Richard Harrington Steve

Richard's theatre credits include *Art and Guff* (Soho); *Stone City Blue* (Clywd); *Unprotected Sex*, *The Snow Queen* (Sherman Theatre); *Gas Station Angel* (Royal Court / tour) and *Nothing to Pay* (Made in Wales). Television credits include *Bleak House*, *The Jewish Revolt*, *Dalziel & Pascoe*, *Silent Witness*, *Holby City*, *Rehab*, *Score*, *Care*, *Tiger Bay* (BBC); *Spooks*, *Hustle* (Kudos/BBC); *Gunpowder, Treason and Plot* (Box TV); *The Hidden City* (Hallmark) and *Coronation Street* (Granada). Film credits include *The All Together* (Establishment Films); *Mathilde* (Film 87); *Joyrider* (Classic Film); *Secret Passage* (Delux); *House of America* (September Films) and *Mule* (Film Four). Radio credits include *And Quiet Flows The Don* and *Night Must Fall* (Radio 4).

Anna Maxwell Martin Hayley

Anna's theatre credits include *The Entertainer*, *Dumb Show* (Royal Court); *His Dark Materials* (for which she was Olivier nominated), *Honour*, *Three Sisters*, *The Coast of Utopia* (National) and *The Little Foxes*

(Donmar Warehouse). Television credits include *Bleak House*, *North and South* (BBC); *Dr Who* (DW Productions) and *Midsomer Murders* (Bentley Productions). Film credits include *Enduring Love* (Roger Michell); *Eddie Loves Mary* (Clandestine Films) and *The Hours* (Stephen Daldry).

Katherine Parkinson Lydia

Katherine's theatre credits include *Flush* (Soho); *Cigarettes and Chocolate* (King's Head Theatre); *The Unthinkable* (Crucible, Sheffield); *The Riot Act, The Increased Difficulty of Concentration* (Gate); *Camille* (Lyric Hammersmith); *Deep Throat Live on Stage* (Edinburgh Assembly Rooms / Fat Bloke Productions); *Frame 312* (Donmar Warehouse) and *The Age of Consent* (Bush). Television credits include *The IT Crowd* (Talkback/Channel Four); *Doc Martin* (Buffalo Pictures/ITV); *Dirty Filthy Love, Ahead Of The Class* (Granada) and *Casualty* and *Extras* (BBC).

Company

Bijan Sheibani *Director*

Bijan won the James Menzies-Kitchin Memorial Trust Award for Young Directors in 2003, for which he directed Harold Pinter's *Party Time* and *One for the Road*, and he won a Mark Marvin Rent Subsidy Award for his production of Edward Bond's *Have I None* in 2002. He was director on attachment at the National Theatre Studio and English Touring Theatre, supported by the John S Cohen Foundation from April 2004 until April 2005. Previous directing credits include *Flush* (Soho); *Breath*, *Party Time*, *One for the Road, The Stoning* (BAC); *The Clink* (Rose Theatre); *Have I None* (Southwark Playhouse); *Summer* (Lion and Unicorn); *Nightwatchman* (Oval Cricket Ground); *Peace for our Time* (Cockpit Theatre); *Hystery* (Embassy Theatre) and *The Lover* (Burton Taylor Theatre). Previous assistant directing credits include *As You Like It* (West End); *A Dream Play* (National); *Terrorism* (Royal Court); *Twelfth Night* (ETT) and *Ryman and the Sheikh* (Tamasha). He has also assisted on two operas: *The Tempest* by Thomas Ades (Copenhagen Opera House) and *The IO Passion* by Harrison Birtwistle (Almeida, Aldeburgh and European Tour).

Paul Burgess *Designer*

Paul's designs include *Shoreditch Madonna, Flush* (Soho); *Switch ECHO* (WUK, Vienna); *Julius Caesar* (Cheshire Youth Theatre); *For One Night Only* (touring); *The Most Humane Way to Kill a Lobster, Cancer Time* (Theatre503); *Much Ado About

Nothing (Globe, sets only); *One for the Road, Party Time* (BAC); *Have I None* (Southwark Playhouse); *Peer Gynt* (Arcola) and *Choked* (tour). Other designs include the first production of Orton's *Fred and Madge* (OUDS, Oxford Playhouse) and various New York fringe shows. Assistant designing credits include *The Ramayana* (National); *Twelfth Night* (Shakespeare's Globe US tour) and projects for Tara Arts. Film work includes five short films shot in Ghana and videos for various theatre productions. Paul has also created installation-based performances for The Arches, Glasgow, and The Junction, Cambridge. As co-founder of Scale Project he has worked on art-theatre crossover projects in Novosibirsk, Siberia and various UK locations. He also teaches design and video-making for the creative and performing arts charity Youth CREATE.

Guy Kornetskzi
Lighting Designer

Guy's designs include *Hortensia and the Museum of Dreams* (Finborough Theatre); *Faster* (Filter Theatre); *This Story of Yours* (New End theatre); *Have I None* (Southwark Playhouse); resident for *The Magnets* (International Pop Band); *Real Dreams, The Identity Multimedia Launch, Dearly Beloved The Musical, Up 'n' Under, St Joan of the Stockyard* (RBC); *Stolen Time* for *Resolution!2002* (MAP Dance Company); *Christmas Concert 2001, Take it from the Top Cabaret Revue, Musical Theatre Department's Agents' Showcase 2001, Christmas concert 2000* (Royal Academy of Music) and *La Traviata* (Opera

Piccola). Guy has also assisted on various projects including ones at the RNT, ROH and ENO.

Emma Laxton
Sound Designer

Emma's designs include *The World's Biggest Diamond, Incomplete and Random Acts of Kindness, My Name is Rachel Corrie, Bone, The Weather, Bear Hug, Terrorism, Food Chain* (Royal Court); *Parade* (Edinburgh Festival); *Maid's Tragedy* (White Bear); *The Gods are not to Blame* (Arcola); *The Suppliants, Party Time/One for the Road* (BAC); *Break Away* (Finborough Theatre), *The Unthinkable* (Crucible, Sheffield) and *My Dad is a Birdman* (Young Vic). Emma was Head of Sound at Regent's Park Open Air Theatre in 2001 and 2002 and is presently Sound Deputy at the Royal Court Theatre.

● soho
● theatre

- Produces new work
- Discovers and nurtures new writers
- Targets and develops new audiences

Soho Theatre is passionate in its commitment to new writing, producing a year-round programme of bold, original and accessible new plays – many of them from first-time playwrights.

> *'a foundry for new talent... one of the country's leading producers of new writing'* Evening Standard

Soho Theatre offers an invaluable resource to emerging playwrights. Our training and outreach programme includes the innovative Under 11s scheme, the Young Writers' Group (15-25s) and a burgeoning series of Nuts and Bolts writing workshops designed to equip new writers with the basic tools of playwriting. We offer the nation's only unsolicited script-reading service, reporting on over 2,000 plays per year. We aim to develop and showcase the most promising new work through the national Verity Bargate Award, the Launch Pad scheme and the Writers' Attachment Programme, working to develop writers not just in theatre but also for TV and film.

> *'a creative hotbed... not only the making of theatre but the cradle for new screenplay and television scripts'* The Times

Contemporary, comfortable, air-conditioned and accessible, Soho Theatre is busy from early morning to late at night. Alongside the production of new plays, it is also an intimate venue to see leading national and international comedians in an eclectic programme mixing emerging new talent with established names.

> *'London's coolest theatre by a mile'* Midweek

● soho
● theatre

Soho Theatre, 21 Dean St, London W1D 3NE
Admin: 020 7287 5060 Box Office: 0870 429 6883
www.sohotheatre.com

The Terrace Bar

The Terrace Bar on the second floor serves a range of soft and alcoholic drinks.

Email information list

For regular programme updates and offers visit **www.sohotheatre.com**

Hiring the theatre

Soho Theatre has a range of rooms and spaces for hire. Please contact the theatre managers on 020 7287 5060 or go to **www.sohotheatre.com** for further details.

● soho
● theatre

Staff

Acting Artistic Director: Jonathan Lloyd

Executive Director: Mark Godfrey

Board of Directors

Nicholas Allott – chair

Sue Robertson – vice chair

Sophie Clarke-Jervoise

Norma Heyman

Roger Jospé

Michael Naughton

David Pelham

Dr Simon Singh MBE

Roger Wingate

Christopher Yu

Honorary Patrons

Bob Hoskins *president*

Peter Brook CBE

Simon Callow

Sir Richard Eyre CBE

Writers' Centre and Education

Writers' Centre Director: Nina Steiger

Literary Assistant: Rachel Taylor

Education and Workshop Officer: Suzanne Gorman

Administration

General Manager: Catherine Thornborrow

Deputy General Manager: Neil Morris

Casting & Artistic Assistant: Nadine Hoare

Assistant to Executive Director: Tim Whitehead

Financial Controller: Kevin Dunn

Book Keeper: Elva Tehan

Marketing, Development and Press

Marketing and Development Director: Jo Cottrell

Development Manager: Zoe Crick

Marketing Officer: Kelly Duffy

Press Officer: Nancy Poole (020 7478 0142)

Marketing and Development Assistant: Vicky Brown

Box Office and Front of House

Front of House Manager: Erin Gavaghan

Box Office and Audience Development Manager: Steve Lock

Box Office Assistants: Colin Goodwin, Paula Henstock, Celia Meiras, Leah Read, William Sherriff-Hammond, Harriet Spencer, Barry Wilson and Natalie Worrall

Duty Managers: Colin Goodwin, Mike Owen, Miranda Yate and Peter Youthed.

Front of House staff: Frank Carson, Indi Davies, Colin Goodwin, Florian Hutter, Samantha Kettle, Daniel Koop, Minho Kwon, Ian Marshall, Harry Scott and Annabel Wood.

Production

Production Manager: Nick Ferguson

Chief Technician: Nick Blount

Chief LX: Christoph Wagner

Lighting Technician: Mark Watts

THE SOHO THEATRE DEVELOPMENT CAMPAIGN

Soho Theatre receives core funding from Arts Council England, London. In order to provide as diverse a programme as possible and expand our audience development and outreach work, we rely upon additional support from trusts, foundations, individuals and businesses.

All of our major sponsors share a common commitment to developing new areas of activity and encouraging creative partnerships between business and the arts.

We are immensely grateful for the invaluable support from our sponsors and donors and wish to thank them for their continued commitment.

Soho Theatre Company has a Friends Scheme to support its education programme and work in developing new writers and reaching new audiences. To find out how to become a Friend of Soho Theatre, contact the development department on **020 7478 0109**, email **development@sohotheatre.com** or visit **www.sohotheatre.com**.

Sponsors

American Express, Angels, the costumiers, Arts & Business, Bloomberg, Getty Images, International Asset Management, TEQUILA\ London

Major Supporters and Education Patrons

Anthony and Elizabeth Bunker • Tony and Rita Gallagher • Nigel Gee • Goldsmiths' Company • The Paul Hamlyn Foundation • Roger Jospé • Jack and Linda Keenan • John Lyon's Charity • The Perberton Foundation • The Foundation for Sport and the Arts • The Harold Hyam Wingate Foundation

Trusts and Foundations

Anonymous • The Ernest Cook Trust • The St James's Trust • The Mackintosh Foundation • The Mercers' Company • Unity Theatre Trust

Dear Friends

Anonymous • Jill and Michael Barrington • Brin and Sian Bucknor • David Day • John Drummond • Madeleine Hamel • Michael and Mimi Naughton • Oberon Books • Piper Smith Watton • Diana Toeman • Jan and Michael Topham • Carolyn Ward

Friends

Thank you also to the many Soho Friends we are unable to list here. For a full list of our patrons, please visit www.sohotheatre.com

Registered Charity: 267234

OTHER HANDS

First published in 2006 by Oberon Books Ltd
521 Caledonian Road, London N7 9RH
Tel: 020 7607 3637 / Fax: 020 7607 3629
e-mail: info@oberonbooks.com
www.oberonbooks.com

A catalogue record for this book is available from the British Library.

ISBN: 1 84002 650 2

Cover image: Getty Images

Printed in Great Britain by Antony Rowe Ltd, Chippenham

For Rod

My sincerest thanks to the following for their help with
the development of *Other Hands*:
Tamara Harvey, Michael Shaw, Jack Thorne, Charlotte
Mann, Jamie Carmichael, Gabriel Winn, Tina and Stuart
Wade, Bijan Sheibani, Nina Steiger, Jon Lloyd and all at
Soho Theatre.

Plus anyone else who had a hand in it. Thank you.

LW, February 2006

Characters

STEVE, 31

LYDIA, 34

HAYLEY, 30

GREG, 45

Scene 1 ✓

LYDIA's studio flat. Late morning.

LYDIA is standing in front of the computer, looking at STEVE. He stands by the door, a motorbike helmet in his hand. The air fizzes.

LYDIA: You've got an hour.

STEVE: Um

LYDIA: What?

STEVE: It's. I can't predict how long it's

LYDIA: How long

STEVE: I mean, it can take longer

LYDIA: Longer than an hour?

STEVE: Well, it. I don't always know till I. Start. How long I'm going to be doing it for is all

LYDIA: Right. Well / I

STEVE: Sometimes it's just thirty seconds or so sometimes and sometimes it's I do try and keep it as quick as possible but

LYDIA: OK

STEVE: But it can take longer and I can't really tell until I, you know, get down to it

LYDIA: Get down to it

STEVE: Have a go

LYDIA: You don't think with your, your experience you should be able to predict

Because I did tell you quite clearly what I wanted on the phone

STEVE: There's lots of

LYDIA: And you are a *professional* so

STEVE: I mean it just isn't possible to

Beat.

LYDIA: I can only afford an hour.

STEVE: Right.

LYDIA: Sorry.

STEVE: No

LYDIA: I should have said on the phone

STEVE: OK

LYDIA: So

STEVE: Well let's give it an hour and see how we go.

LYDIA: OK.

STEVE puts his helmet down and moves towards the PC.

STEVE: It's the modem, you said

LYDIA: God, I don't know, I mean

God knows what's going on in there just won't connect to the internet

STEVE: Since

LYDIA: Monday

STEVE: OK well let's

LYDIA: I might not be using the right words, the terminology

LYDIA is still standing in front of the PC, barring STEVE's way.

STEVE: Can I

LYDIA: Um

STEVE: Have a look?

LYDIA: Um, yeah

LYDIA starts to move away, then darts back to stand between STEVE and the computer.

Sorry

STEVE: What?

LYDIA: Sorry I just

Thing is I can't let you *start*, you see, because

If you start and then we get to the end of the hour and it isn't fixed, and you. I'm not questioning you know, but. If it isn't fixed and you go away, or it's worse because I don't know, you've run some kind of programme on it and now it's worse it's made all sorts of crawlies come out of the. I mean I'm not saying you would, you know, but

I mean then I'm

Then I'm *really* stuck

STEVE: Yeah

LYDIA: I really need it, I

STEVE: Yeah. Yeah

LYDIA: And you, you did say that. You know, sometimes, doesn't it, it takes more than an hour you said and I can't afford it because

And you can't tell, can you, with people, sometimes it's an hour and five minutes and you get charged for the second hour, for breaking into it but I really

I mean, when I say I can't afford it it's not that I think it *shouldn't* take longer than an hour, like I'm opposed to the idea of paying for this this service that you do, which I actually think is a great idea and you know it's a godsend for people like me so it's not that I don't agree with the idea of paying more than forty pounds it's just that

I mean I just don't have it, I really can't.

I'm sorry

STEVE: No, I

LYDIA: I should have said before

STEVE: No

LYDIA: 'Stead of making you come all the way over here from

STEVE: Fulham

LYDIA: Fulham. Oh, not too far

STEVE: Not too far, no

LYDIA: Quite direct on a bike I should thi

STEVE: I, um

LYDIA: I'm sorry. I really am.

Beat.

STEVE: I could

LYDIA: Yes?

STEVE: You could just pay me for the hour and I'll. I'll stay till it's done.

LYDIA exhales. Smiles.

LYDIA: Yes. Yeah. Thank you

She moves away from the PC.

You see that's. That's kind. That's *kind*

Thank you.

STEVE: Sure.

STEVE sits down at the PC. He flexes his fingers.

LYDIA: So what if it's less than an hour?

STEVE: What?

LYDIA: Joke. Sorry, joke. Just, joke.

STEVE smiles. LYDIA sits down on the bed.

STEVE: You don't have to stay with me if you

LYDIA: It's a studio

STEVE: Right, sorry

LYDIA: Unless you'd like a cup of tea, or

STEVE: No thanks

LYDIA: Or water or

I think I've got some squash, some kind of weird combination like strawberry and apricot or

STEVE: I'm OK.

LYDIA: Don't know why I bought it really, sounds disgusting. Not very grown-up, is it, squash?

STEVE moves the mouse, then frowns.

STEVE: Does it always crash like this?

LYDIA: Oh. Yeah, always. All the time. Hit 'save' every five seconds now.

STEVE: You work from home, do you?

LYDIA: No, I. No.

Pause. STEVE reboots the PC. LYDIA watches him.

God, you must. You must really see some stuff

Things people have on their machines

STEVE: Don't really look

LYDIA: No?

STEVE: Not really interested

LYDIA: No

Beat.

No? You must be a little bit?

STEVE: Maybe a / bit

LYDIA: A little bit. Curious.

STEVE: Most people there's not

LYDIA: Well you won't find any porn on there

LYDIA laughs and looks away.

STEVE: What you do with your personal

LYDIA: My *personal*

STEVE: It's none of my business

LYDIA: I don't have anything *personal* on

STEVE: I'm just here to fix it

Beat.

LYDIA: There's someone I email, OK?

And if. If I can't email, then

And I haven't been able to email for days so I feel a bit

STEVE: OK

LYDIA: But I wouldn't

I wouldn't want you to read any of the emails, so

STEVE: I won't

LYDIA: I haven't met him

I

It's ridiculous really, but

STEVE: I won't

LYDIA: Read them, no

STEVE peers at the screen.

STEVE: Shit

LYDIA: What? What?

STEVE: I'm going to be here a while.

Fade.

Scene 2 *? a section?*

GREG's office. Late afternoon.

GREG and HAYLEY are drinking coffee from vending-machine cups. GREG is emptying sachets of sugar into his.

HAYLEY: You don't seem convinced.

GREG: I'm not.

HAYLEY: I'm afraid the board are.

GREG: Seduced, aren't they?

Flashy logos, big words. Sugar?

HAYLEY: No thank you

He offers her a sachet.

GREG: Sweetener?

HAYLEY: No

GREG: Sweet enough

HAYLEY: I like it bitter

We're going to have to work together

GREG: Oh I know

HAYLEY: And an atmosphere, we've found, an atmosphere of hostility can only serve to make the process more

GREG: Painful

HAYLEY: Less comfortable for your department, the staff. If they see that you're

GREG: Hostile

HAYLEY: Uncomfortable

Because what we're doing really isn't it's not a revolution it's just

Incremental change that will rationalise

GREG: Feels like a revolution

HAYLEY: Because it's new and it's not familiar

If we work together, we can turn it round.

GREG takes a sip of his coffee and pulls a face.

GREG: Christ. Get them to put in a new coffee machine I've never managed to get that changed

HAYLEY: This really isn't a reflection on your

When you've been in something so long, it's hard to step back and have a look, isn't it, see the big picture. Impossible for anyone to know how to fix something that

GREG: They all think they're going to lose their jobs, you know. People coming to me every five minutes, 'Are there going to be job losses?'

HAYLEY: There may be opportunities to *upskill* the labour force and

GREG: They feel watched, you know, what can I say to that? Threatened

HAYLEY: But if for example we were to incentivise

GREG: Incentivise like I have to do such and such hit such and such a target if I want to keep my

HAYLEY: Not you personally. Your position's safe, you're fine

GREG: Yours as well, I presume, what've you got riding on this?

HAYLEY: I don't think that's

GREG: Be sad if you lost that snazzy little motor, what is it, little sporty thing?

HAYLEY: TVR

GREG: Good er, handling?

HAYLEY: It roars I like it.

GREG: Flashy

HAYLEY: What do you drive?

GREG: I sometimes

I sometimes look at, you know, someone like you and I think what do you know, really? What do you know about any of this, how young you are, you've never

HAYLEY: It isn't a case of

GREG: I started out stacking shelves, you know.

HAYLEY: Assistant Manager, wasn't it?

GREG looks at her.

HR file

GREG: It was a small branch. They gave you my file?

HAYLEY: I'm doing a Human Performance Review, I have to understand the humans involved

GREG: And I'm not under threat?

HAYLEY: No

> The company's always had a strong policy of rewarding loyalty, long-term service, always has. But sometimes that isn't all / you

GREG: Are you saying

HAYLEY: It's possible we have the specialist knowledge

GREG: I don't?

HAYLEY: And the time, we have time, I mean with all the things you have to do do you have time to do this kind of project?

GREG: I'd cost less

HAYLEY: With all the, just the day to day, keeping an eye on the day to day, whereas we have the time and the objectivity and the expertise to

> *GREG's mobile rings.*

> D'you want to

GREG: No, no, it's

HAYLEY: I don't mind

> *GREG looks at the phone.*

GREG: Bloody hell

> *He picks it up.*

> Yes love. Yes, I'm in a. Can't you handle it, I'm in a

> What's wrong with him?

> His what? What kind of. Do they look

> Is that him in the. Put him on the phone. Because I might be able to

> Well if you had to ring me at work. Will you just put him on the phone, so I can see what's. Thank you.

> *GREG looks at HAYLEY.*

HAYLEY: Everything alright?

GREG: My son's being

> Jonathan? Mum says you won't do your homework.

> What's wrong with your hands? What kind of

> Where? What your wrist, or fingers or

> Have you taken. OK. Well it should, half an hour it should kick in

You know what this is, don't you? It's that bloody X-Box, that's what it is, isn't it? How much homework have you

OK, give it half an hour for the Nurofen to kick in, OK, then get on with it, I'll be home at what, half seven, I want to see your Maths finished and on the kitchen table, yes?

Or you won't be going out with your mates for the rest of the month, that's what. OK? Put your mother ba

Jonathan has hung up. GREG puts the phone down. Looks at it. Presses a button to switch it off.

(*To HAYLEY.*) Don't have kids.

HAYLEY: I might one day

GREG: Stay as you are

Says his fingers hurt so he can't do his homework. Lazy sod.

Boy doesn't seem to have any idea what he wants to do with his life

HAYLEY: How old?

GREG: Fifteen

HAYLEY: Well, *fifteen*

Did you know at fifteen?

GREG: Wasn't so much choice back then

Did you know?

HAYLEY: Didn't know what a management consultant was when I was fifteen

GREG: I'm still not sure

HAYLEY: You've done well for yourself, even if it's not what you thought / you'd

GREG: I mean I'm still not sure what a management consultant is

Beat.

I'm baiting you, being hostile

HAYLEY: Noted

GREG: You can put it in your report

HAYLEY: I'm sorry this is difficult for you. The company's been very slow to get consultants involved, you've got peers in other companies that've been working with people like me for years they're quite used to it, don't see us as a threat at all

23

GREG: So we're backward

HAYLEY: No

There *is* room for more *forward-thinking*

GREG looks at her.

So

OK

We'll be on site from Monday, have a look at processes as they stand, progress it from there. Um. There'll be a couple of consultants and a team of analysts working into me and they'll / be

GREG: 'Working into'?

HAYLEY: Um

GREG: (*He mimes a wriggling worm with his finger.*) 'Working *into* me'

HAYLEY: Working *for* me, then

GREG: Sounds a bit

Rude

HAYLEY: Well, they'll be here, my team, so if you could accommodate them that / would be

GREG: Won't you be here?

HAYLEY: I'll be in and out, I'll be around

Perhaps if you and I sit down together again in a week or so, touch base then, then we'll be in a position to actually leverage

GREG: 'Leverage', isn't it?

HAYLEY: Sorry?

GREG: Don't we pronounce it 'leverage' in this country?

HAYLEY: I

GREG: Bet you say 'oriented', not 'orientated' as well, don't you?

HAYLEY takes her Palm Pilot out of the laptop bag at her feet.

HAYLEY: It's an American consultancy, there's a culture

GREG: Leverage

HAYLEY: Shall we look at schedules?

GREG: 'Schedules'

HAYLEY: How's next / Wednesday?

GREG: I don't do my diary, my secretary

HAYLEY: Or Thursday morning? Friday afternoon?

HAYLEY slides the Palm Pilot out of its case with a little effort. GREG looks at the case and picks it up.

GREG: Broken.

HAYLEY: Yes, I.

You know, how you get. Used to things

GREG: What d'you mean?

HAYLEY: You know, something gets broken and I

I never have time to you know, fix it properly so it gets sellotaped and then you kind of modify your behaviour and you get used to the sellotape and

You get used to it being broken, you adapt.

GREG looks at her.

/ Not with a project, with personal / Cut

GREG: You let your guard down for a second then

HAYLEY: It won't happen again.

GREG: I rather liked it.

HAYLEY looks at her coffee. GREG leans back in his chair.

Fade.

S:obj:

H obj:

Hayley tries to initiate a convo.

Scene 3 ✓

Kitchen/Living area of HAYLEY and STEVE's flat. Evening.

STEVE is on the Playstation. HAYLEY is unpacking groceries from a plastic bag on the counter.

HAYLEY: Huh

STEVE: What?

HAYLEY: Bread-bin

STEVE: On the counter

HAYLEY: I know, but

We never put the bread in it, do we, we always put the bread next to it. Why do we do that?

STEVE: I'unno

HAYLEY: I mean, that's

She starts to put the new bread inside the bread-bin.

I'm putting it inside, OK?

No answer.

Steve, the bread's in the bread-bin, OK?

Looking inside the bread-bin.

Last year's green bagel is no longer in the bread-bin, it's in the bin.

She puts the old bagel in the bin, then looks in the bread-bin again.

This is disgusting. There's crumbs in here from when we moved in. Was it my mother got us this or yours?

No answer. She wipes inside the bread-bin with a cloth.

You know, you could unplug yourself and talk to me. Ask me how my day was

STEVE: How was your day?

HAYLEY: Doesn't count

STEVE: What?

HAYLEY: You have to have taken your hands off the controls and turned the screen off

STEVE: I'm nearly

HAYLEY: And be facing me

HAYLEY boils the kettle and prepares a mug for tea.

STEVE: Just finish this level

HAYLEY: You could ask me how my big meeting was

STEVE: How was your meeting?

HAYLEY: He was a wanker. Greg the wanker

STEVE: Everyone you work for's a wanker.

HAYLEY: You know the weirdest thing happened to me on the way home tonight. The weirdest thing. Coming back from work and I was driving, the same way I always drive, like every day and

I got to a junction, lots of little roads going off it and. God, I suddenly I couldn't remember which way I was going, which way was home. The same way I go every day, like on autopilot but suddenly

Like the light was different or. Or I was different. I don't know

STEVE: Shit

HAYLEY: What?

STEVE: Died

HAYLEY opens the fridge.

HAYLEY: Oh, *Steve*

STEVE: What?

HAYLEY: There's no fucking milk. Did you finish the milk?

STEVE: Sorry

HAYLEY: You couldn't have

STEVE: You just went to the supermarket

HAYLEY: There was loads this morning

STEVE: I drank some

HAYLEY: You could have called me I mean

STEVE: Hayley, it's

You know, calm down

HAYLEY: Well when did when did we get so bloody inefficient?

STEVE: Over-reaction

HAYLEY: I don't think it is

Beat.

Sorry, I'm tired

Got to go to this party.

STEVE: Fuck, is that tonight?

HAYLEY: I've got to socialise with these people it's. You know, if I'm trying to make partner next year. It's important

STEVE: OK, so we're going

HAYLEY: I am. You you said you didn't want to

STEVE: No, I'll come

HAYLEY: OK.

HAYLEY gets the ironing board and the iron out of a cupboard and sets them up. She goes out of the room and returns a moment later with a pair of trousers and a top. She irons the trousers during the following.

What did you do today?

STEVE: I did a job

HAYLEY: Did you?

STEVE: Woman in Putney. Viruses. Rebuilt it from scratch

HAYLEY: God, how long did that

STEVE: 'Bout six hours

HAYLEY: God, so that's (*Adding it up.*) two hundred and / forty

STEVE: Forty

HAYLEY: Yes, two hundred and forty

STEVE: Forty. I got forty pounds.

HAYLEY: For six hours?

STEVE: She. She only had forty pounds so we made a deal

HAYLEY: Steve, your first job in a week and you made a

STEVE: She wanted to sort it out before I started and I didn't know if it was going to take six hours or six minutes, so

And I was

HAYLEY: What?

STEVE: She really needed it

HAYLEY: What for work?

STEVE: No, I don't know for. Some bloke she was emailing

HAYLEY: What, a boyfriend?

STEVE: She hadn't met him

HAYLEY: You made a deal so she could play the fucking personals?

STEVE: She was really upset

HAYLEY fiddles with the controls on the iron, frowning, half watching STEVE.

HAYLEY: D'you know how this fucking

No of course you don't

HAYLEY pours water into the iron.

Was she pretty?

STEVE: Lonely, I think

HAYLEY: Everyone's lonely

STEVE looks back to his game, picks up the handset.

Forty pounds isn't

For a week

You'd get more on the dole. You'd get more on the fucking game, Steve, even with your complete lack of

There's a vacancy at work. IT Support Manager

Thirty grand starting salary

STEVE: No

HAYLEY: We'd see more of each other

STEVE: I left, we had a cake. Said 'fuck it' on the top

HAYLEY: 'Fuck I.T.', wasn't it?

Six hours for forty pounds. Hope she gave you a cup of tea

STEVE puts the handset down and flexes his fingers.

Did you call the doctor?

STEVE: Just stiff from doing that job

HAYLEY: Playstation

STEVE: No, it's not

HAYLEY: It's the only repeated action you do. Just go to the doctor, get it sorted.

You know you don't get any sympathy until you get it looked at

HAYLEY finishes ironing the trousers and changes into them. STEVE goes to the fridge.

If you're coming we've got to go

STEVE: Yeah

STEVE takes a can of Fanta out of the fridge. He opens it, drinks, then looks at HAYLEY, who is frowning.

Alright

STEVE takes a glass from the cupboard and pours some Fanta into it. He watches the froth go down, intently. Sees HAYLEY watching him again.

What?

HAYLEY: I still don't know how you work. All this time. How your brain works.

STEVE: Bit of a fucking mystery yourself.

HAYLEY: Kiss me.

STEVE makes a kissing sound with his lips. He goes back to sit at the Playstation. HAYLEY prepares to iron her top, stretching it out on the ironing board to smooth out creases. STEVE flexes his fingers. HAYLEY sees this.

You don't have to come if it's hurting.

HAYLEY picks up the iron and knocks the plastic water jug to the floor.

Dammit

She picks it up from the floor, then irons the top. It's quite a complicated garment.

STEVE: You don't want me to come

HAYLEY: Put your shoes on

STEVE: You asked me to come

HAYLEY: Yeah, but

STEVE: You asked me last week

HAYLEY: You said you didn't want to

STEVE: I said I didn't want to, it doesn't mean I'm not going

HAYLEY: Well you should have made it clear 'cause I've got used to the idea of you not coming now

And I've arranged to meet Nick off the Tube.

STEVE: He won't mind

HAYLEY: I would

STEVE: Yeah but you're

HAYLEY: What?

STEVE: I dunno

HAYLEY: Well if you're coming put your shoes on

You're wearing that, yeah?

STEVE: What would you like me to wear?

HAYLEY: Just. That's fine, what you've got on

STEVE: I could wear the black / one

HAYLEY: It's fine it's just a house party

STEVE: Where are my

HAYLEY: There

STEVE: Where?

HAYLEY: By the sofa

STEVE: No, not the

HAYLEY: You're not going in your trainers, god

STEVE: You said it was just a house / party

HAYLEY: Please, for me, just wear your nice shoes

STEVE picks up the shoes and sits down on the sofa. He puts them on carefully.

And don't tell any jokes

STEVE: Which one's Nick?

HAYLEY: Nick from work Nick

STEVE looks at HAYLEY.

You've met him

STEVE: All look the same

HAYLEY: You talked about Doom

STEVE: OK

HAYLEY: Then you told him the stupid 'how we met' story

STEVE: He probably asked

HAYLEY: Yeah no, I remember

About half way through I looked at us, like from a few steps away and I realised we were being really irritating. This routine telling it the exact same way and it's really not the greatest story is it not really and I fucking hate that

STEVE: What?

HAYLEY: With couples when you talk to them or discussing something with them and you can tell they've had the same conversation before they're just doing it again, we've started doing that

STEVE: We can talk to people separately.

Pause. HAYLEY puts her top on.

HAYLEY: You know I think I might stop

I might just *stop talking* 'cause everything I say feels like I've said it before every fucking thing sounds like I've rehearsed it I just have to open my mouth and I piss myself off

31

STEVE: You shouldn't

HAYLEY: What?

STEVE: Everyone gets

HAYLEY: Do they? I'm even less special than I thought

You ready?

She sees STEVE having trouble with the laces on his shoes.

Steve, you can't even do your laces, you've got to go to the doctor. 'Cause don't think I'll be here when it gets to not being able to wipe your own arse.

STEVE: It's fine

HAYLEY kneels down and starts to tie STEVE's shoe-laces.

HAYLEY: Let me / do it

STEVE: You don't have to

HAYLEY: I'm not being sympathetic I'm trying not to be late we've got to go

STEVE: My trainers are Velcro so

HAYLEY: Yep

HAYLEY finishes tying the laces.

OK. Handbag

HAYLEY picks up her bag and coat.

Come on

They go out into the hallway. A moment.

HAYLEY comes back in.

Wait. Wait.

She unplugs the iron and winds the cord up neatly and tucks it into the handle.

Two seconds.

She puts the iron and the board away, then looks around at the room. She is still for a moment.

Steve?

STEVE: (*Off.*) Yeah?

HAYLEY: I want to sleep with someone else.

Pause. STEVE comes back and stands in the doorway.

STEVE: Who?

HAYLEY: I don't know yet.

Fade.

Scene 4 ✓

LYDIA's studio flat. A week later. Late afternoon.

STEVE and LYDIA face each other, as at the start of Scene 1.

LYDIA: Nice to see you

STEVE: I can't stay today

You know, if it takes

If it takes longer than however long you

LYDIA: No, I can afford you today. And it's nice to see you

I've said that.

LYDIA smiles.

STEVE: So, um

LYDIA: It's the printer

STEVE: Oh

LYDIA: It won't. Print

STEVE: Right

LYDIA: Obvious, really, I mean that's all I need it to do

I've got to get. Got to start applying for a job and there'll be CVs and letters and. So I'll need it

STEVE: Thing is I don't

Don't really do printers

LYDIA: Oh

STEVE: Mostly there's enough in the handbook to sort it out if there's something not working

LYDIA: I just assumed it's all

STEVE: And if the handbook doesn't help then usually you just replace it, get a new one

LYDIA: Oh god

STEVE: 'Cause they're not that expensive so there's usually no point fixing them, you just get a new one

LYDIA: I've only just worked out how this one works

When it's working

STEVE: See most of them these days they've got a built-in obsolescence, they're designed to only last a few years so

Have you looked at the

LYDIA: Handbook

STEVE: Yes

LYDIA: Think I've lost it

STEVE: Have you, sorry if this is obvious, have you done stuff like checked the paper tray, checked it's got ink, that sort of

LYDIA: It tells me, on the little display when it's, when it needs paper, or. Gives the illusion of being user-friendly

I'm sorry, I didn't know you didn't do

STEVE: What's it say now?

LYDIA looks at the display on the printer.

LYDIA: Machine Error 41

STEVE frowns.

I know, I mean, what does that mean, you know?

STEVE: Probably says in the

LYDIA: Handbook, yeah

Beat. They look at each other.

STEVE: RTFM

LYDIA: Sorry?

STEVE: Geek-speak. Read The Fucking Manual.

LYDIA smiles.

Have you looked online?

LYDIA: Didn't think of that

STEVE: Give it a try

LYDIA: I don't suppose, since you're here, you couldn't

I know it's not your remit really but you'll still know more about it than I do and

cut STEVE: OK

LYDIA pulls the computer chair out for STEVE to sit on.

LYDIA: Thank you

STEVE goes to sit down at the computer.

STEVE: But this is working, yeah?

LYDIA: Oh yes. Yes. No problems at all, thank you

Haven't actually used it that much this week

STEVE: I thought it was really

LYDIA: Yeah. Well. We were emailing every day, now we're not so

Now we're not at all.

We were arranging to meet each other, then he just stopped

Beat. LYDIA goes to the kitchen.

You know, I wasn't lying last week when I said I couldn't pay more it's just I

LYDIA returns with two glasses of squash.

got a new credit card.

STEVE: No, I didn't mean to

LYDIA puts one of the glasses down next to STEVE.

Thanks.

It's just my girlfriend's on my back about undercharging people so

LYDIA: Course. Course she is.

LYDIA smiles weakly. STEVE looks at the squash.

STEVE: You don't um, happen to have a straw at all

LYDIA: A straw?

STEVE: Drinking straw

LYDIA: Oh. Yeah, think so

LYDIA goes to the kitchen to look.

You know, when I said it was nice to see you I meant, I didn't mean

I was just I was so glad you helped me, felt like I was going mad.

STEVE: Yeah

LYDIA: Surrounded by all this stuff and I don't know how any of it works, the computer and the CD player, can't even work out how to change the ring tone on my phone so it pisses me off every time it rings, not that it rings very often, all these microchips all these passwords and PIN codes

LYDIA comes back with a straw. Hands it to STEVE.

I mean I just don't feel *equipped*

STEVE: Yeah

STEVE puts the straw in his squash.

LYDIA: Like at school in Physics they taught us how to wire a plug, but that's about as far as I

STEVE bends down to drink his squash through the straw. LYDIA watches him, distracted for a second.

Um

STEVE goes back to looking at the screen.

And things come with fitted plugs now anyway, so.

STEVE: Here we go, there's some stuff on here…

LYDIA goes to stand beside him.

LYDIA: And like, when I get another job. If

I've only been out of work four months but they've probably changed the technology since then so I've got another photocopier to make friends with, work out what the fax means when it beeps at me

STEVE: Yeah.

STEVE glances at LYDIA, then back at the screen.

LYDIA: I had a good job

She looks at her hands.

STEVE: What was it?

LYDIA: Office Manager

STEVE laughs.

LYDIA laughs.

I know. Brilliant, isn't it?

LYDIA looks out of the window, stops laughing.

I loved it, actually

Then I took my first two-week holiday since I'd started there and some consultants came in, shook things up

By the time I came back they'd realised they didn't need an Office Manager, hadn't missed me at all. Turned out they could um, manage.

What's she like, your girlfriend?

STEVE: Why?

LYDIA: Curious

STEVE: She's. Efficient. Always pre-heats the oven.

She likes air-fresheners, every room in our house smells different. Never room to plug anything in, all these little plastic gel things

They smile at each other. STEVE looks back at the screen.

It's fatal

LYDIA: What?

STEVE: Error 41. You'd have to replace the

How long have you had it?

LYDIA: Three years?

STEVE: Thing is after that long it's out of warranty, anyway, so to replace the print-head that's going to cost you like

Well you might as well get a new one

LYDIA nods.

Sorry.

LYDIA: Get one on the credit card, then

STEVE: Tottenham Court Road

LYDIA: Right

STEVE: Lots of places along there, see if you can get a two-year warranty on it.

LYDIA: D'you think they'll see me coming? Red light on the door that flashes when a clueless bit of fluff walks in?

STEVE: You're not clueless, most people don't

LYDIA: Yeah, I guess.

STEVE stands.

So

STEVE: I should

LYDIA: Let me find you some money

    LYDIA fishes in her purse and pulls out two twenty-pound notes.

    Forty pounds

    She hands it to him.

    Thank you.

    You know, people like you, people who know how to do stuff, you

    You make me feel *possible.*

STEVE: Didn't fix it, did I?

LYDIA: It's not just

    Beat. They look at each other.

    Um

    There's something else I need you to do, would you mind?

STEVE: Um

LYDIA: Just a second.

    LYDIA goes to the kitchen. STEVE rubs the back of his head. LYDIA comes back carrying an electric kettle. She puts it on the table between them. STEVE looks at it. Then at LYDIA.

STEVE: I, um

    STEVE clears his throat.

    I don't do kettles

LYDIA: No. Course not. Stupid.

    I'm sorry, I'm trying to

    I read a book this week which I really shouldn't do because I get so sad when I get to the end

    And

    Pause.

STEVE: What's um

    What's wrong with it?

LYDIA: Won't boil water

STEVE: Right

LYDIA: Which is actually all I / need it to do

STEVE: Need it to do, yeah

Have you tried the fuse?

LYDIA: Yeah, I can do plugs.

STEVE: You changed it?

LYDIA: Yes

STEVE: You might have to just buy a new one. Argos, or

LYDIA: I know how to buy a kettle.

STEVE: Course.

STEVE swings his backpack onto his back. He has a sudden burst of pain in his hand.

Ah *fuck.*

LYDIA: God, you OK?

STEVE: Yeah, I

LYDIA: Sit down

STEVE: No, I. Shit.

LYDIA: God, can I help can I do anything?

STEVE looks at LYDIA.

Would you like a drink? I mean, go for a drink?

Pause.

STEVE: I, um

LYDIA: No. Yeah. No, that was a better idea before you got here, actually. Didn't seem so. I had this idea that maybe

Is your hand OK?

STEVE: Yeah.

LYDIA: I've completely cack-handled this

STEVE: No

LYDIA: Just thought maybe we could go out for a drink.

STEVE: Um, when?

LYDIA: Um, now?

STEVE: OK.

LYDIA: OK.

STEVE holds his hand up.

STEVE: Mine's a pint. With a straw.

LYDIA laughs.

Fade.

Scene 5

Evening. GREG and HAYLEY are eating dinner in a Chinese restaurant.
GREG is frowning at HAYLEY's drink.

GREG: And that's a drink, is it? *Bubble* tea

HAYLEY: Try a bit?

She offers him her straw.

GREG: Got something floating in the bottom, blob of something

HAYLEY: Tapioca balls

GREG: That supposed to be there?

HAYLEY laughs.

HAYLEY: Yes

They're chewy

Want a bit?

GREG: No I

Drinks with bits in, I don't

HAYLEY: Taste of the future

GREG makes a face and goes back to his noodles. HAYLEY laughs.

Listen thanks for this afternoon, what you said in the meeting

GREG: Well I realise I. I think before I may have made it seem like I thought you didn't know what you were doing

HAYLEY: Yes

GREG: Like I thought you were too young to

HAYLEY: Yes

GREG: And now, having worked with you I realise

I think I was possibly *rude*

HAYLEY: Yes

GREG: Brusque

HAYLEY laughs.

HAYLEY: Good word.

Well thank you.

GREG: Still not convinced by the rest of them

HAYLEY: They'll win you round

GREG: Silly haircuts

HAYLEY: Well the good thing about the rest of them is they all answer to me

GREG: There we go then

HAYLEY: There we go

GREG: Here

GREG takes a small package out of his suit pocket and hands it to HAYLEY. HAYLEY looks at him, questioning.

Little something. Personal

HAYLEY picks up the package and starts to open it.

HAYLEY: I'm intrigued

Thank you

It's a case for her Palm Pilot.

GREG: For your PDA

HAYLEY: Yes. Thank you

GREG: You didn't replace it already

HAYLEY: No

HAYLEY takes her Palm Pilot out of her jacket, which is draped over the back of her chair, and replaces the broken case with the new one.

There we go, look

GREG: Quite snazzy

HAYLEY: Thank you, that was really

Thank you

GREG: Is your hand OK?

HAYLEY: My

GREG: Your hand – you made a face when you took the case off

HAYLEY: Oh

> Just a little twinge

GREG: Getting old

HAYLEY: Pulled a muscle or something it's fine

> *GREG sits back in his chair, looks at HAYLEY. She puts the Palm Pilot into her jacket pocket, smiling.*

> We can go back to baiting each other now if you like

GREG: Your turn

HAYLEY: We don't have to.

GREG: Would you say you were happy?

HAYLEY: Is that baiting?

GREG: No

HAYLEY: That's a very personal / question

GREG: It's a very simple question

HAYLEY: I don't think

GREG: I'm not violating any kind of code or

> I didn't ask what colour knickers you're wearing

> Just, are you happy?

> *GREG's phone rings.*

HAYLEY: D'you want to

GREG: No

> *He looks at the caller display. It's his wife.*

> God no.

> *He switches it off.*

> You married?

HAYLEY: No

GREG: It's hard work

HAYLEY: I'm in a long-term committed / thing

GREG: How long?

HAYLEY: Eight years

GREG: Try twenty-one

> You didn't answer my question, are you happy?

HAYLEY: Yes

GREG: Not just OK, not just yes because you're a failure if you're not.

Actually *consciously* happy.

Beat.

HAYLEY: Are you?

GREG: For example – when you walk in, at home

HAYLEY: Yes

GREG: And you see your what, boyfriend, partner?

HAYLEY: Boyfriend

GREG: At the end of the day when you see him, are you happy?

HAYLEY thinks.

HAYLEY: Yes.

Yes I'm always happy to see him

It's just sometimes I'm pretending.

GREG: Oh yes. That one

HAYLEY: Yeah?

HAYLEY picks up some food with her chopsticks but drops it half way to her mouth.

Not very um, dextrous today

GREG: Shall we get you a fork?

HAYLEY: Yeah.

They look around for the waiter. GREG sees him across the room and tries to catch his eye but fails.

GREG: Ever feel like you're being ignored?

HAYLEY smiles.

Probably scared I want to complain about the bits in your drink

He gets up.

HAYLEY: Greg / it's fine

GREG: Not a problem

GREG goes to find a fork. HAYLEY watches him go, then takes her Palm Pilot out of her jacket pocket and looks at it, smiling. She sees GREG returning and replaces it hurriedly, knocking her jacket off the back of the chair as she turns round. GREG sits down and hands her a fork.

HAYLEY: Thank you

GREG: So not happy

HAYLEY: Oh

I don't know

GREG: Hang on your jacket's

GREG stands and picks the jacket up, then puts it on the back of HAYLEY's chair carefully.

Tell me about him

HAYLEY: It's not

Yes it is about him. Probably.

HAYLEY picks up her fork and starts to eat.

God, that's better. That's easier

Last week I

Last week for the first time I noticed the noise he makes when he kisses me

GREG: Fatal

HAYLEY: And you know he'd never, like just now with my jacket he'd never do that. Wouldn't even notice. And I think maybe I want someone who

Just the watching out the uncalled-for little things like that

But I can't just say, can I? That I'd love him more if he carried my bag I mean what does that sound like?

I mean even to me it sounds

And anyway once you've *asked* it's not

GREG: Yes

HAYLEY: And I don't know when I started to think like that, like a few years ago I

It's like I'm changing but not *actually* you know there's no actual or circumstantial

Just things I think changing. The way I think

Like the other day I'm on the train to Slough or Maidenhead or

GREG: Somewhere fun

HAYLEY: And I bought the paper and I read this article about um, tiger prawns, did you know this?

GREG: No

HAYLEY: Tiger prawn farming it's like, it's this really big problem it's
apparently it destroys the land, the the the *mangroves* in Vietnam
and Thailand and places like that they cut all the mangroves
down so they can farm these shrimp. But then the chemicals and
stuff they feed to them because of that level of acid or whatever
going into the soil it kills it, the um the earth is after a few years
it's worthless it's completely spent so when the shrimp farming
fails, when all the shrimp die which apparently happens quite a lot
or the crop gets contaminated or whatever, they can't go back to
farming anything else. But no-one tells them that so all this land
gets used up 'cause demand's got so big and everyone wants all
these poor farmers to grow tiger prawns not rice or whatever so
the economy's going to shit in these countries because we all like
tiger prawns so much

GREG: I don't really like prawns

HAYLEY: OK well

GREG: Carry on

HAYLEY: So I read this in the morning and then by about eleven
when I'm starting to get hungry for lunch all I can think about is
fucking tiger prawns, how much I want a tiger prawn sandwich so
I'm scouring Marks and Spencers in Slough or

GREG: Maidenhead or

HAYLEY: Somewhere bollocks and I'm just absolutely desperate for
a tiger prawn salad you know. After reading that. And I think what
does that

And then I'm not sure if I care

Like fox hunting

Like I know I'm I'm opposed to fox hunting I know I must be I just

I can't remember why

GREG: OK

HAYLEY: And sometimes you know, sometimes I think I'd really like
to *wear fur*

Pause. GREG laughs.

For example.

HAYLEY laughs.

GREG: You're brilliant

HAYLEY: Am I?

GREG: I think so

   I do, you're so

HAYLEY: I'm just permanently I don't know *baffled*

GREG: Good word

HAYLEY: I'm thirty already, you know?

GREG: Well, *thirty*

HAYLEY: I mean I don't think it's like an age crisis just. You know, *thirty*

GREG: But everyone feels like that, don't they? Whatever age

HAYLEY: Do they?

   HAYLEY sits back in her chair.

   So what are they doing, are they all just coping?

GREG: I suppose.

HAYLEY: It's commonplace

GREG: I'm not saying you're not having a difficult

HAYLEY: Happens all the time

GREG: You don't

   People like you don't

   Don't happen all the time.

   Fade.

Scene 6

Putney High Street, 1:00 AM.

STEVE is moving away from a cashpoint, clumsily trying to slide some notes into his wallet. He's in the middle of telling LYDIA a story. LYDIA stands a few paces off, listening to STEVE, a little wobbly. They're having a nice time.

STEVE: So basically by then she's so desperate she tells me, like right in the middle of this open-plan office, she tells me if I can get the file back she'll not only love me forever she'll also take me out for dinner that night

LYDIA: And you did

STEVE: You know, I'm sat there thinking if I can string this out a bit longer she'll offer me a blow job

LYDIA giggles.

I got the file back, yeah

Tried to make it look a bit difficult, you know, but it's just sat there in the Recycle Bin

Anyway she did take me for dinner and she was so relieved about the file she got a bit drunk and we accidentally ended up shagging and then here we are

Eight years later.

Beat.

LYDIA: Four five seven nine

STEVE: What?

LYDIA: Four five seven nine

STEVE: D'you want to shout it a bit louder?

LYDIA: Sorry

LYDIA giggles.

Sorry

All that forty pounds just on drinks

She sees he's still having trouble with the money.

You alright there?

STEVE: Yeah, I

LYDIA: Here

She takes the wallet and slides the cash into it for him.

I'm not going to nick it

What is it, arthritis or

STEVE: You looked over my shoulder

LYDIA hands the wallet back.

LYDIA: Can't help it

STEVE: You're not supposed to look, it's

LYDIA: I don't usually tell people

STEVE: But you usually look?

LYDIA: Can't help it

She staggers slightly.

God, I'm a bit

Nice that bar, isn't it?

STEVE: Yeah

LYDIA: Will you be in trouble?

STEVE: What?

LYDIA: At home, being home so late. Missing the last tube

STEVE: She'll be asleep. Might not notice

STEVE looks back at the cashpoint.

LYDIA: What is it?

STEVE: I'll have to change it now

LYDIA: Change what?

STEVE: PIN number

LYDIA: Oh come on

STEVE: You might tell someone

LYDIA: I won't

STEVE: No offence but I'd feel a bit

LYDIA: You won't change it because it's the same PIN number you've
    had since forever and there isn't another four digits in the world you'd
    trust yourself to remember without having to write it down. Right?

God I'm actually

STEVE: What?

LYDIA: You stopped being laid-back for a second there

Beat.

STEVE: I should grab a taxi

LYDIA: Can I get in it with you?

Drop me home

STEVE: OK

LYDIA: Stop me from shouting your PIN number in the street, won't it?

STEVE looks around for a taxi.

D'you have a joint account, you and Hayley?

STEVE: Yeah

LYDIA: Do you?

STEVE: Yeah. Not for, not for everything.

I mean, this wasn't

LYDIA: No. What d'you use it for?

STEVE: Joint things, the flat, bills, that stuff

LYDIA: You don't pay your income into it?

STEVE: Uh-uh. She earns a fuckload more than me, so

LYDIA: D'you think you'll stay together, you two?

STEVE: Never know, do you?

STEVE puts his hand out for a taxi, which sails past.

Shit

LYDIA sits down on the kerb.

LYDIA: If you could be more something, what would it be?

STEVE: More

LYDIA: You know like more intelligent, more rich more happy

STEVE: More

More, um

I don't know, more

LYDIA: Articulate?

LYDIA laughs.

Sorry

STEVE thinks.

There must be something, some ambition, something you want

STEVE: Um

LYDIA: Or like something you had and you'd like it back, something you used to do that doesn't happen anymore

LYDIA looks at STEVE, then away.

I used to dance, years ago

STEVE: Yeah?

LYDIA: I mean, I used to go to places like clubs and. Places where you dance. And now I don't even go to those places and even if I did I probably wouldn't dance now

LYDIA stands.

Is she. Is it everything you've ever wanted?

STEVE: It's fine

LYDIA: Fuck Steve, it's *fine*?

STEVE: You just

LYDIA: What?

STEVE: I don't know you get to a stage where it's all OK, you know it just carries on and it's OK

LYDIA: Which is exactly what you want a life that's *OK*

STEVE walks away a few paces.

I'm sorry I've been

I mean I realise I am I realise I can be a little bit *irritating*

STEVE: No

LYDIA: That would be my 'less' thing. Less irritating

I um. I haven't been out of the house in a week. So I'm a bit giddy. And I don't usually drink alcohol at home 'cause drinking on your own's so

Actually, I'm lying, I have been out – on Tuesday I went to the supermarket down the road with my sunglasses on at like seven at night. Oh, and then on Thursday I got so fed up with my own company I just left the flat, like when people have an argument and one of them just walks out of the house and slams the door I wanted to be that person. But then I was on the street and I didn't really have anywhere to go and no-one to go back into the house and hug sorry so I went to the newsagents to fucking *browse*

LYDIA looks at STEVE. He's clutching his hand and wincing.

You alright?

STEVE: Not brilliant

LYDIA: Get you a taxi

She looks around. There aren't any. Looks back at STEVE.

Oh, you poor thing

She puts her hands around his and strokes them.

STEVE: What would you be more of, what's your 'more' thing?

LYDIA: Oh, um. More brave. Braver

STEVE: Yeah

LYDIA looks away, then at STEVE. She takes his hand and plants a slow kiss on his palm. She looks up at him.

Sorry, my wrist

LYDIA smiles and goes to kiss the inside of his wrist. STEVE takes his hand away.

No, I mean. Ow. Sorry, it hurts

LYDIA: Sorry

STEVE: Sometimes they're numb or they tingle or

They're tingling, like they're *full* of something it's so

LYDIA: It's got cold, you should probably keep it warm

LYDIA takes her scarf and wraps it around STEVE's hands. She takes a piece of paper from her pocket.

I've um. This is my phone number

She puts the piece of paper in his pocket.

Just, you know. Since I've nothing else for you to fix

She looks around for a taxi.

Fade.

Scene 7

HAYLEY and STEVE's flat. Late morning.

STEVE is sitting at the kitchen counter eating a yoghurt through a straw. He isn't holding the pot, so it skids a little on the work surface. HAYLEY watches him, holding a pile of leaflets.

HAYLEY: So there's lots of things it could be, they gave me all these

She lays the leaflets out on the counter.

Repetitive Strain Injury, apparently it's usually some kind of repeated action, not always it doesn't have to be that

As STEVE gets to the bottom of the yoghurt pot the straw makes a slurping noise.

There's lots of different sorts

Carpal Tunnel Syndrome

Rheumatoid arthritis

STEVE: You took the morning off

HAYLEY: Tendinitis

STEVE: To go to the doctor for me?

HAYLEY: Tenosynovitis

You weren't going to do it

Tennis elbow

Your elbows are fine, aren't they?

STEVE: Just my hands

STEVE slurps the yoghurt again. HAYLEY frowns. She snatches the pot away from him, cuffing one of his hands as she does so.

Ow

STEVE holds his wrist.

HAYLEY: I didn't do that.

STEVE: Sudden movement it

HAYLEY puts the pot in the bin.

Ow

HAYLEY: Oh, look

Holds a leaflet towards STEVE.

Potential risks of computer games and text messaging, there you go.

STEVE: You didn't have to go for me

HAYLEY: I know

Must be love

And you won't take the herbal things I got

STEVE sits down.

The symptoms are kind of the same for most of them so

You look at the treatment rather than the cause, apparently

STEVE: What's the treatment?

HAYLEY: Um, keeping still

You'll be alright there / then

STEVE: Keeping still, that's it?

HAYLEY: Ice-packs make it hurt less

STEVE: Right

HAYLEY: And you mustn't let it get too hot or that makes it swell up more

STEVE: Ah

HAYLEY: What?

STEVE: Been keeping it warm

HAYLEY: You see this is why you should have

(Mimicking her 'nagging' voice.) nya nya nya

STEVE: What else?

HAYLEY: Anti-inflammatory drugs, Nurofen, ibuprofen stuff

STEVE: Not strong enough I've been / taking them

HAYLEY: You've

You didn't tell me

STEVE: Just 'cause I didn't tell you doesn't mean I'm not doing anything

Don't work anyway

HAYLEY: Well you can get stronger ones from the doctor

HAYLEY hands him a pharmacy package.

Like these

Thank you, Hayley

STEVE doesn't take them.

It's this or cortisone shots and I'm not doing that for you I hate needles

HAYLEY swaps the package from one hand to the other, wincing slightly. STEVE frowns.

STEVE: How'd you get a prescription?

HAYLEY puts the package down.

HAYLEY: Begged and pleaded

Must be love

STEVE: Hayley

HAYLEY: What?

STEVE: You can't have got a prescription for me, surely

HAYLEY: Maybe I shagged the doctor

I got ice-packs

HAYLEY takes four ice-packs out of a plastic bag.

STEVE: Only got two hands

HAYLEY: Two to use and two to keep in the freezer, isn't it?

They're not ice right now, obviously, they have to go in the freezer for a bit so

HAYLEY pulls the freezer door open. She winces and holds her wrist.

Tsss

STEVE looks at her.

Fine

Beat.

Fine. Probably just sympathy pain

HAYLEY closes the freezer door with her hip. She meets STEVE's eye.

So I've got sympathy twinges.

STEVE: Is it both?

HAYLEY: Right one's worse

STEVE: Fingers or

HAYLEY: Fingers, wrist

STEVE: Shit

HAYLEY: I didn't get it to piss you off

I'll just take a couple of days sick, rest up

It's been stressful so

STEVE: Work

HAYLEY: Yeah, did you notice?

What?

STEVE: You didn't actually take the morning off for me, then

HAYLEY: Well no I

No.

HAYLEY goes to sit on the sofa.

STEVE stands looking at her, then around the room, unnerved at having her there during the day. HAYLEY sits on the sofa looking ahead, her hands in her lap.

STEVE: So you're just going to

HAYLEY: Waiting for the ice-packs

STEVE: Right

HAYLEY: That alright with you?

STEVE: Course

HAYLEY: Anything you'd like to say? While we're here?

STEVE: I don't know, sorry?

HAYLEY: It's not your fault it's not bloody infectious is it?

> *Beat.*

> D'you want any lunch?

STEVE: No

HAYLEY: Because I can't be bothered to / make any

STEVE: I had some. Didn't think you'd be here

HAYLEY: What did you have?

STEVE: Soup

HAYLEY: God, Steve

> D'you know what's happening?

STEVE: No

> *STEVE goes to sit on the sofa next to HAYLEY.*

HAYLEY: You don't have to

STEVE: What?

HAYLEY: Nothing it's fine

> *They both look ahead.*

STEVE: So what's your repeated action, then?

HAYLEY: I don't know, repetitive strain of putting up with you?

STEVE: Don't say that, kiss me

> *HAYLEY looks at STEVE.*

> What?

HAYLEY: I don't tingle anymore

> I used to

> To tingle

STEVE: My hands tingle

HAYLEY: Yeah, my hands tingle just not

    Everything I feel feels like it's in my hands

    Rest of me's totally

STEVE: Numb

HAYLEY: You know, when we first started you were the sun on my face

STEVE: Kiss me

HAYLEY: Now the sun is the sun on my face

    Beat.

    Fucking hurts, doesn't it?

    Fade.

Scene 8

LYDIA's studio flat. Late morning.

STEVE and LYDIA face each other. There are no objects between them.

STEVE: I thought maybe, you know

    Maybe you might need some help with your toaster

LYDIA: No, toaster's fine

STEVE: Or the dishwasher or

LYDIA: Haven't got one

STEVE: Right

    OK

LYDIA: It's all fine

STEVE: Did I

LYDIA: What?

STEVE: Have I done something wrong?

LYDIA: No. No

    Just

    Surprised to see you

    Haven't seen you in, what

STEVE: Don't know

LYDIA: Three weeks

    Something like that

STEVE: / Sorry

LYDIA: No, it's fine, how are you?

STEVE: I'd have come sooner but

    I've been really

    Can't do anything, can't ride my bike I walked here today

LYDIA: And your phone's been cut off

STEVE: No, it

LYDIA: Joking, just a joke

STEVE: The keys are hard, the buttons

LYDIA: Right

STEVE: Had to completely stop typing, can't work at all

LYDIA: God, that's

    I'm really sorry

STEVE: No

    LYDIA smiles.

LYDIA: Nice to see you

    As usual

STEVE: Yeah

LYDIA: I wasn't sure if I would

STEVE: No?

LYDIA: After, you know, after

    You know

    You kind of disappeared a bit

STEVE: Sorry

LYDIA: No, I'm

    STEVE is cradling his left hand.

    Are they hurting?

STEVE: Bit

LYDIA: Would it

Can I help keep them warm?

STEVE: No

LYDIA: No

STEVE: Not because

LYDIA: No?

STEVE: 'Cause it turns out cold is better. Ice-packs and

LYDIA: Right. Should've taken more notice in Biology

STEVE: They wouldn't have taught

LYDIA: No I suppose not

STEVE: At that level

Pause. They're standing very close.

LYDIA: I've got ice in the freezer or peas or

STEVE: OK

LYDIA: OK.

LYDIA goes to the freezer and takes out a packet of frozen peas.

These are in a packet so. Keeps it contained not like ice in a plastic bag rattling around, leaking and

Which one, is it both or

STEVE: Yeah

LYDIA: I've only got the one

STEVE: This one's worse

LYDIA: OK

She applies the packet to STEVE's left hand.

STEVE: I don't want to

LYDIA: What?

STEVE: Make them go bad, melt and

LYDIA: I never eat peas it's fine. Don't know why I've got them. I've got a tin of beans as well somewhere, never going to eat it. Coconut milk in a can I mean I wouldn't know where to start you know?

That better?

STEVE: Yeah.

LYDIA takes STEVE's right hand and uses it to hold the packet in place. She moves away, laughs a little.

What?

LYDIA: I kind of missed you

STEVE: Yeah?

LYDIA: Funny how someone can

People get important, you know?

STEVE: Um

LYDIA: Then they go away

STEVE: I should've

I didn't realise

LYDIA: No, that's

No reason why you would

I don't have many people around so I get a bit silly about people

STEVE: Right

LYDIA: And quite often I frighten them off

STEVE: OK

LYDIA: So I thought I might have frightened you off

And you probably don't you probably don't need anyone and

I mean god knows what I'd *add*

STEVE: I wasn't frightened I was just

LYDIA: Poorly, yeah

Sorry I'm just

Kind of explaining how I get silly about

I mean when you came in today when I opened the door I had this *physical*

Beat.

I had such a lovely time the other week. When we went out.

STEVE: Me too

STEVE looks away.

LYDIA: Are you OK?

STEVE: Yeah, I

LYDIA: Something wrong?

STEVE: Things are a bit

At home

LYDIA: D'you want to tell me?

STEVE shakes his head, still looking away. Pause.

D'you know what would be OK?

STEVE: What?

LYDIA: If you'd come round because

Because you kind of needed a hug

Beat.

That would make me really happy you know, if

If you'd needed a hug and you'd come to me

Pause.

STEVE: I

LYDIA: Doesn't matter

How's your hand?

STEVE: I don't know what to

LYDIA: We could just forget I said anything

STEVE sits down on the bed. He puts his head in his hands.

STEVE: Ow

LYDIA looks at the frozen peas.

LYDIA: That's probably defrosting now I should probably

She sits down by STEVE and takes the packet from his hand.

STEVE: I did

LYDIA: Did what?

STEVE: Because I needed a hug

LYDIA: You don't have to say that

STEVE looks away again.

Steve

Oh

LYDIA goes to put her arms around STEVE.

STEVE: But gently 'cause I do really hurt

LYDIA strokes his back.

LYDIA: How's that?

STEVE: Yeah

LYDIA: Lie down

Come on you need to

I won't kiss any of you and if you happen to cry I won't say anything

STEVE lies on his side on the bed, his hands in front of his face.

STEVE: They look weird, wrong, they look like someone else's

LYDIA: Shh

LYDIA strokes his hair.

How's that?

STEVE: Yeah

I could sleep

LYDIA: I like that

STEVE closes his eyes. LYDIA lies down behind him and continues to hold him. The room darkens as STEVE falls asleep, until it is lit only by the blue light from the computer screen. A moment of painless quiet.

LYDIA carefully sits up. She looks at STEVE and smiles. She looks over at the computer. She gets off the bed carefully and creeps over to sit at the computer. She types a couple of words then looks over to check if it has woken STEVE. It hasn't. STEVE starts to snore. LYDIA giggles to herself. She goes back to the screen and types quickly, checks what she's written and is satisfied. She switches on the printer. It makes a succession of scraping and scratching noises as it calibrates.

Dammit.

LYDIA tries to switch it off, but it won't oblige.

Shut up shut up. Shh

STEVE wakes up and the room is fully light again. LYDIA turns to see him.

Sorry. I'm sorry

It's new I'd forgotten it makes such a noise

STEVE: 'S OK

STEVE sits up, accidentally leans on his hand as he does so.

Ow

LYDIA: Ooh

OK?

STEVE: Yeah

LYDIA: I didn't mean to wake you, sorry

STEVE: What you doing?

LYDIA: Job application

Sudden burst of energy

Last day for getting it in today and it looks like it might be perfect so

STEVE rubs his eyes.

Turns out you snore

STEVE: Yeah

LYDIA: I'm a light sleeper

LYDIA turns back to the computer.

I'm going to say I used this five months to improve my computer skills. So it doesn't seem such a big gap. Teach myself all the stuff, spreadsheets and

STEVE looks at the printer.

STEVE: Nice printer

LYDIA: Yeah

STEVE: You installed it

LYDIA: No. That um, superstore place. They send a chap round with the delivery. Really helpful.

STEVE stands up, awkward.

STEVE: Cool

LYDIA: Are you embarrassed?

STEVE: No

LYDIA: 'Cause you fell asleep

STEVE: No, not

STEVE sits back down on the bed.

Just now I had this, I've had it before but lying here I had this

The toaster was

LYDIA: The toaster?

STEVE: Yeah

LYDIA: My toaster?

STEVE: No, mine at home it

LYDIA: This is a dream?

STEVE: Yeah. Yeah

Whenever I put anything in it it disappeared out the bottom

Not onto the floor or

Like there was some kind of black hole, an abyss or something.

Beat.

LYDIA: Let me take you home

STEVE: Take me home

LYDIA: Yes

STEVE: I'm not sure I

LYDIA: You need looking after

Not medically, just

STEVE: I don't want to go home

LYDIA: You've kind of got to go home, Steve. It's where you live

I'll look after you.

Fade.

Scene 9

Coffee bar. Early afternoon.

GREG and HAYLEY sit facing each other. He has a cappuccino, she has an iced coffee with a straw. They smile at each other, easy.

HAYLEY: Did you know infinity's not the biggest thing anymore?

GREG: No

HAYLEY: They found something bigger

GREG: What?

HAYLEY: Don't know

It was on the train last week, going to Slough or

GREG: Swindon or

HAYLEY: Somewhere fun. And there's some bloke opposite me reading the New Scientist or something and on the front the headline was 'Infinity – not the biggest thing'.

Makes you think, doesn't it?

GREG: Yeah.

HAYLEY: Made me laugh. And I thought about telling you when I saw it, I sort of turned to you as if you were (*She gestures to the space beside her.*)

I wanted to tell you.

So we should get back to the office, really

GREG: You wouldn't like to sit here flirting a bit longer?

HAYLEY: Would you?

GREG: Give me your hand

HAYLEY: I can't

GREG: Why?

HAYLEY: Hurts to move it *-she can't feel-*

GREG: Alright

whole scene begins
Imagine I'm holding your hand

HAYLEY: OK

That's

Surprisingly nice

GREG: Surprisingly?

HAYLEY: Nice surprise, I mean

GREG: You like it

HAYLEY: Yeah

GREG: Good

GREG sits back in his chair.

Side of your nose

HAYLEY: Greg

GREG: Tell me that isn't nice

HAYLEY: It's

GREG: Surprisingly nice

HAYLEY: Yeah

GREG: Which side?

> *HAYLEY closes her eyes, tilts her head to the left slightly.*

HAYLEY: That side

GREG: There

> Where now?

> *HAYLEY tilts her head the other way.*

HAYLEY: That side

GREG: Yes

> There.

> *HAYLEY leans forward.*

HAYLEY: What else?

GREG: Your bottom lip

HAYLEY: God

GREG: I want to…suck your bottom lip

HAYLEY: God

GREG: Too much?

HAYLEY: I

> No, not too much

GREG: Sure?

HAYLEY: Just

> New

> Feels different   *never had something meaningful*

> *Beat.*

GREG: Hot, isn't it?

> *GREG smiles.*

HAYLEY: Your face, you're so naughty

GREG: I want to I want to suck your finger

Each one of them in turn and lick the palm of your hand and a line up your arm, pushing your sleeve back a little and lick the inside of your elbow

And I want to put my hand on your stomach, touch your skin

HAYLEY: God

GREG: And

No, your turn

Beat.

HAYLEY: OK, I

I'm not very

GREG: Go on

HAYLEY: OK

I want to…run my fingers through the short hair at the back of your neck

GREG: Uh-huh

HAYLEY: Starched line of your shirt collar

And

And slide my hands around your waist, underneath your jacket

Untuck your shirt at the back, run my fingers along

GREG: I want to put my tongue through the holes between the buttons in your shirt

HAYLEY: And you do these tiny little kisses down the side of my neck

GREG: I want to stand behind you, holding you close round your waist so you feel me hard against your arse

HAYLEY: All the time with these tiny little kisses

GREG: And I want to undo the buttons on your shirt, slide it off your shoulders

HAYLEY: Facing me, your eyes and my eyes and your hands in the back of my hair

GREG: And bite your shoulder

HAYLEY: Bite my shoulder?

GREG: Gently. It'll be nice

HAYLEY: Your hands in the back of my hair and stroking my hair

Pulling me to you

GREG: And then undo the button on your trousers and slide the zip down

HAYLEY: Your hands either side of my face

GREG: Slide my hand inside

HAYLEY: Kissing my eyelids

GREG: Before you expect me to

Make you shiver with the surprise

Slide my hand into your pants

HAYLEY: Knickers. God, are we at knickers already?

GREG: I don't know, are we?

HAYLEY looks at GREG, thinking. A moment. She bends down slowly to take a sip of her iced coffee. GREG watches her.

Christ, even when you

Just watching you drink coffee makes me

HAYLEY looks away.

Are you

HAYLEY looks at GREG.

HAYLEY: Put your hand inside

GREG: Inside your knickers?

HAYLEY: Do it

GREG: OK. Sliding my hand inside

HAYLEY: Yeah

GREG: My finger between your legs into your cunt

HAYLEY: Pussy

GREG: Your pussy

HAYLEY: Are you happy with pussy? I don't like cunt

GREG: Pussy

And your hands around my

HAYLEY: Dick

GREG: Really?

HAYLEY: What d'you prefer?

GREG: Cock, I always think

*Different generations
new relationship.
learning eachother*

HAYLEY: I always think cock sounds a bit gay

   Beat.

GREG: Little bit of sweat on your forehead

HAYLEY: And I pull you into me

GREG: Already?

HAYLEY: I want you in me

GREG: I won't last long

HAYLEY: Want to feel you that close to me

   I don't mind if you don't last long

GREG: Push into you harder and harder

HAYLEY: Slowly

   But really deep

GREG: My head against your shoulder

HAYLEY: Looking into my eyes and we're moving and our eyes are *locked*

GREG: And you feel it

   You feel it

   You really feel like you're being *fucked*

HAYLEY: Fuck

GREG: What?

HAYLEY: I

GREG: What?

HAYLEY: No, carry on

GREG: What's wrong?

HAYLEY: Don't stop now Greg, you're so close

GREG: You're crying

HAYLEY: I'm not crying

GREG: What is it?

HAYLEY: I'm not crying

   I

GREG: What?

HAYLEY: I feel like I'm really being *fucked*

GREG: Let's go somewhere

HAYLEY: What?

GREG: Let's go somewhere

A hotel or

HAYLEY: Greg

GREG: Yes

HAYLEY: I'm crying

GREG: Yes

HAYLEY: I started crying and you want to take me to a hotel

Beat.

Greg I can't

GREG: I know

HAYLEY: *You* can't

GREG: You know, we both can

HAYLEY: Yes I know

GREG: D'you want to?

HAYLEY: I'm crying

GREG: Because you want to or because you don't want to?

HAYLEY: I don't know

GREG sits back in his chair.

GREG: You don't know.

HAYLEY looks away.

HAYLEY: You know I've been having this thing

GREG: Yes

HAYLEY: These thoughts about maybe

You know

HAYLEY looks at her lap.

But

It's like

I don't know, like I thought I could just go for a little walk

Just a little wander around, look at stuff, the scenery

GREG: Men

HAYLEY: Other men yes

GREG: The the grass is / greener

HAYLEY: Oh my god the grass isn't just greener I mean it's got ten-foot sunflowers I can I can *smell* them if sunflowers smell, I don't know

GREG: Right

HAYLEY: I mean it's almost it's almost unbearable being able to smell it and all because of the

The stupid walk, just this thinky little walk looking at the scenery 'cause when I started I just wandered around a little while and it was fine it was pleasant I could see stuff and then

Because all of a sudden I realised I'd actually wandered to the top of a cliff

Like the walk up to it had been like this, really flat

She gestures to demonstrate the gradual incline of the hill then clutches her arm.

Tss. Twinge, sorry

Sorry

So it's pretty flat really only a little bit of a hill then all of a sudden I get to the edge of this cliff and there's water below it and I'm standing looking down at these waves and I'd never meant to be there I'd just gone for this thinky little walk

And some of me's thinking god, this is interesting I mean most of me's terrified but a lot of me's thinking bloody hell this is interesting

You know?

GREG: And what happens next in the dream, do you

HAYLEY: It's not a dream it's a metaphor it's

I'm contemplating jumping

GREG: Really?

HAYLEY: Yeah. Because it looks good and exciting down there and

But then I start to worry I'll stand too close to the edge, I'll stand on a piece of loose rock and it'll crumble and I'll lose my footing and then I'll fall. Because of standing too close and thinking about it.

And then – what? I'm in the sea and there's no ladder back up and this is assuming the fall and the impact hasn't killed me or I haven't landed on a rock or something but what if I can't climb up?

GREG: You don't have to climb back up.

HAYLEY: But I can't just

    Greg, I can't swim

    I can't do it.

    I'm sorry.

    Fade.

Scene 10

Kitchen/Living Room area of HAYLEY and STEVE's flat. Afternoon.

LYDIA sits on the kitchen counter, her legs crossed. STEVE sits on a stool, his arms on the counter, bent, his hands starting to claw. There's a plastic bowl beside them full of nearly melted ice-lollies.

LYDIA: So I'm standing in the kitchen this morning making a cup of tea and the freezer it. It audibly exhaled, like it let out this long sigh

    Like it was breathing

STEVE: Sigh of relief

LYDIA: Dunno

STEVE: (*The lolly-sticks.*) How they doing?

LYDIA: Nearly melted

    LYDIA lifts a stick out of the bowl.

    Yeah, some of these are done

    She puts the stick back and licks her fingers.

    Bit sticky, have to give them a wipe

    I couldn't think of anything but lolly-sticks that'd work

STEVE: No

LYDIA: And then I tried to think where I could buy the sticks without lollies on them and

STEVE: Not obvious

LYDIA: I couldn't think of anywhere.

    And I've no idea how we get them attached to your fingers

STEVE: Bandages

    The front door slams, off.

LYDIA: Is that

STEVE: (*Calling.*) Hayley?

STEVE looks at LYDIA.

LYDIA: Just introduce me, it's fine

HAYLEY comes into the kitchen. She leans on the doorframe.

STEVE: You alright?

HAYLEY: Yeah fine who's this?

STEVE: This is my friend Lydia

HAYLEY: Hi

LYDIA: Hi, nice to meet / you

HAYLEY: How d'you guys

LYDIA: Steve fixes my computer I'm hopeless

HAYLEY: Are you sleeping with her?

STEVE: Am I

HAYLEY: Sleeping with her

STEVE looks at LYDIA.

Are you having sex with her?

STEVE: Oh no. No

HAYLEY: Steve's clients often try to have sex with him

STEVE: No they

HAYLEY: The women

Most of your clients are hopeless women, aren't they?

STEVE: Some of them

HAYLEY: He's an absolute godsend

LYDIA: I don't want to sleep with him

HAYLEY: No, I wouldn't recommend it. Not 'cause I'd punch you or anything just 'cause he's cr

STEVE: Hayley

Pause.

Are you pissed?

HAYLEY: Apparently you know, apparently if you drink fizzy alcohol through a straw it makes you more drunk

Which, you know, which is some consolation

STEVE: It's half past four

HAYLEY: Pubs are open.

(*To LYDIA.*) Did he tell you he's given me RSI?

Sorry, not RSI, I think mine's Carpal Tunnel Syndrome d'you know what that is? The big nerve gets *squeezed*

HAYLEY looks at STEVE.

Injury or over-use

(*Looks at the bowl.*) Oh you made orange soup

LYDIA: Melted um

HAYLEY: It's what?

LYDIA: Melted ice-lollies

HAYLEY: Is it

Why?

No, I don't care actually

LYDIA: We were going to make a splint for Steve's hand

HAYLEY: A splint. Marvellous

STEVE: Why you home?

HAYLEY: I'm sick I don't have to work if I'm ill

I'm going to have a drink I think

STEVE: Hayley

HAYLEY: I'm going to have some milk if there is any is there any milk Steve?

STEVE: Yes I th

HAYLEY: Marvellous

HAYLEY opens the fridge door using a strap. She takes out an unopened carton of milk.

Ooh a new one good behaviour what have you done?

STEVE: Nothing

HAYLEY tries to open the carton without success.

HAYLEY: Ow fuck

Can't get this fucker / open now

LYDIA: Here

LYDIA takes the carton and opens it for HAYLEY.

HAYLEY: Ooh she's good isn't she good?

See why you like her, darling, Mrs Fixit.

HAYLEY looks at LYDIA.

I know you

LYDIA: Do / you

HAYLEY: How do I know you?

LYDIA: I don't

HAYLEY: I definitely recognise you

LYDIA: I don't think

HAYLEY: You look so

LYDIA: Just one of those faces, I think

HAYLEY: No, I'm sure I

HAYLEY looks at the sink.

You did the washing up

STEVE: Lydia did it

HAYLEY: Did she now

LYDIA: Sorry, I

Someone once came and did my washing up once when I had flu
and it was nice so

HAYLEY: Did Steve do it

LYDIA: Steve

HAYLEY: Your washing up

LYDIA: No. Not Steve

HAYLEY: No. Wouldn't have been Steve.

Pause.

LYDIA: (*To STEVE.*) I should go

HAYLEY: No no no, in my own house, I'll do the going

I am going to another room

She turns to go. Turns back.

With

The milk

She picks up the carton of milk in both hands and goes out the door. STEVE looks at LYDIA.

STEVE: She's not like that, she's never like that

LYDIA: I'm. I'm going to go

STEVE: You don't have to

LYDIA: Come on, I'm in the way

STEVE: Please

Beat.

LYDIA: I do know her

Beat.

The job I had

Hayley was one of the consultants who decided I probably shouldn't have a job

STEVE: Shit

I'm sorry

LYDIA: No it's fine

I probably wouldn't remember me either

STEVE: I'll talk to her

LYDIA: It's done now

It was months ago, she

There's other stuff you need to sort out, Steve

You need to do something

STEVE: Don't go

STEVE leans in to LYDIA, tries to kiss her. She backs away.

LYDIA: N

No

Steve

STEVE: Sorry

LYDIA: No

Beat.

You do need to do something I don't think it's *that*

Starting some stupid thing with me isn't

LYDIA looks away, then looks around the room.

You told me Hayley likes air-fresheners

STEVE: Yeah

LYDIA: I think they must have all run out 'cause it smells Steve

STEVE: It smells

LYDIA: Stinks. Coming in from outside

LYDIA bites her lip.

That was ridiculous what you just did

STEVE: Sorry

LYDIA: I should

I should just walk away

STEVE: I'm sorry. I'm sorry

LYDIA: You need to talk to her

STEVE: I'm crap at

LYDIA: You need to sort it out

STEVE: I know. I'm crap

LYDIA: No, Steve, you can't just

You can't just say that and be crap

It's not enough to just identify that you're crap and then always be that, you know?

I'll call in a couple of days, OK?

STEVE: OK

LYDIA: OK.

LYDIA leaves. STEVE goes to the kitchen cupboard, which he opens by using a strap around the handle, and takes out an aerosol can of air-freshener. He frowns, trying to work out how he can operate the can with his physically impaired hands. He solves it by placing the can on a

surface and pressing the spray button with the flat of his hand. He starts to move around the room, spraying the air, upholstery etc. HAYLEY comes in and leans on the doorframe, slightly sobered up. She watches him.

HAYLEY: She gone, your little friend?

STEVE: Yeah.

STEVE looks at HAYLEY.

HAYLEY: You going to tell me off for drinking all the milk?

STEVE: D'you feel bad?

HAYLEY: Not really.

STEVE sprays.

STEVE: She lost her job.

HAYLEY coughs.

HAYLEY: You trying to as

You trying to asphyxiate me with that?

STEVE: Smells in here

HAYLEY: Why don't we just open the window?

STEVE looks at HAYLEY.

What?

STEVE: She lost her job 'cause of you.

HAYLEY: Can we just

STEVE: Did you hear me?

HAYLEY: Steve, the window?

STEVE: I can't open it I can't turn the catch

You sacked her

HAYLEY: I didn't sack her I don't

We don't say 'sack' it's not

HAYLEY remembers.

Ohhhh

Ohhh *her*

God, yeah, god that company was a mess I *knew* I recognised her

STEVE is looking at her.

What?

77

STEVE: D'you feel bad? At all?

HAYLEY: Steve

STEVE: You didn't even remember

HAYLEY: It was months ago, project before last

STEVE: She went on holiday and when she got back

HAYLEY: Has she got a new job?

STEVE: No

HAYLEY: No efficiency

STEVE: Takes more than / efficiency to

HAYLEY: Yes it takes a bit of fucking gumption

Look at you, all sorry for her

STEVE: I don't think it's right

HAYLEY: No, well

STEVE: Or fair

HAYLEY: Oh no, definitely not fair

Not fair that I get to be the evil one either

STEVE: I don't think

HAYLEY: That your loyalty or whatever the fuck

That you would assume that I'm the

STEVE: I'm not saying

HAYLEY: And can I just point out while we're at it that the proceeds of my wicked life are going a fair way to funding your completely ineffectual one right now and I haven't heard the slightest bleat of dissent about it from you before?

STEVE: My friend lost her job 'cause of you I'm feeling a bit

HAYLEY: People lose their jobs 'cause of me all the time, you just never met one before.

What d'you want me to do about it? Apart from kill myself.

STEVE: Help her

HAYLEY: Oh fuck off

STEVE: Why not?

HAYLEY: If I go back on, now if I

STEVE: There's no room for

HAYLEY: For what?

STEVE: I don't know

Kindness

Beat.

HAYLEY: Get a job, Steve. Then we'll have a chat about *helping*

STEVE: I've got a job.

HAYLEY: It's not a job, it's an excuse.

Did she tell you what she did? Why I remember her out of the hundreds of lives I've terrorised?

STEVE: You didn't remember her / I had to

HAYLEY: I was drunk, I remembered her in the

Did she tell you what she did?

STEVE: I don't

HAYLEY: She didn't tell you what she did here's what she did

Will you stop doing that while I

STEVE stops spraying.

Big company, kind of place you only know the people on your floor, only those faces and that makes, that can make a company vulnerable that kind of bigness

Means you have to go the extra mile with some things

Security for example

Be extra alert, promote alertness

There'd been thefts a a a *spate* of thefts, computer equipment, hardware going missing and one of the things we

STEVE: She didn't steal anything

HAYLEY looks at STEVE.

What?

HAYLEY: You're very sure of what she is, what she's like

STEVE: Well I

HAYLEY: Are you sure you're not fucking her?

STEVE: I'm not

HAYLEY: You seem to have attached some kind of

STEVE: I'm not fucking her

HAYLEY: She's incredibly important all of a sudden

STEVE: She's got no-one to

HAYLEY: Can I carry on?

> She's coming back into the office one day, been out for lunch and

> Some bloke in some kind of generic IT-support T-shirt's struggling to get through the door with an armful of hard drive

STEVE: Right

HAYLEY: So she helps him

> She holds the door open for him and he smiles and she doesn't check his badge

> She gets back to her desk and there's nothing on it

> *Beat.*

> Y'know, she held open a door for a man stealing *her* computer

> They're supposed to be on *special alert*, she just stands there, holds the door open, lets it happen

STEVE: But anyone could've

HAYLEY: She should have recognised it anyway, covered in stickers apparently, pictures of dogs

STEVE: But everyone

HAYLEY: No, Steve, not everyone. Why is it OK to fuck up like that?

STEVE: It's a big company, *one* computer

HAYLEY: When they're looking to *rationalise* the *headcount* they're going to take stuff like that on b

STEVE: She'd never do it again though, would she? Once you've done something like that

HAYLEY: It's very sad. There it is.

STEVE: It's not just sad it's

> Her life is shit

HAYLEY: Really

STEVE: She lives in this basement, crappy little bed-sit

HAYLEY: Bed-sit or studio?

STEVE: Studio whatever it's fucking depressing

HAYLEY: Lots of people / live in

STEVE: D'you know she told me the other day that I am currently the most important person in her life

Me.

Imagine what a shit life that is.

Beat. HAYLEY looks at STEVE. She laughs.

HAYLEY: Poor fucker

STEVE: So I think we should help her.

HAYLEY: She can't go back there, we restructured there's no

STEVE: You could put in a word somewhere

You could call someone

HAYLEY looks away.

Or something

You could do something

Fade.

Scene 11

GREG's office. Afternoon.

There's a bunch of sunflowers on the desk – still in Interflora wrapping, but the kind of bouquet that stands up by itself, without needing to be transferred into a vase.

GREG is sitting looking through a report, writing notes in the margin with a pencil. HAYLEY comes to the door.

HAYLEY: Hi.

GREG sits back in his chair and looks at her, then points at the sunflowers.

GREG: From you?

HAYLEY: I thought they looked friendly

GREG: No note.

HAYLEY: It would only have said I'm sorry and I wanted to sa

To *say* it

GREG looks at her, waiting.

I'm sorry.

GREG: From the other side of the fence, are they?

HAYLEY: I'm sorry.

GREG: Do you always say it with metaphorical flowers?

Did you want to discuss something?

Beat. HAYLEY takes a deep breath.

HAYLEY: I *am* going to have to stop working on the project

GREG: Right

HAYLEY: As expected

GREG: You don't have a special word for

HAYLEY: What?

GREG: 'Stop working on' it's not very

Not very *jargon* is it

HAYLEY: I don't

GREG: Don't we have anything to leverage today

HAYLEY: Greg

GREG: No *caveats* to *rationalise* or *incentivise* or

No *tools* to help us out of this funny

HAYLEY: No

GREG: Everything's a tool, isn't it?

HAYLEY: You're being a bit of a tool, Greg

GREG: You're abandoning my project

HAYLEY: Not abandoning

GREG: Pulling out

HAYLEY: It's in safe hands

GREG: Silly haircuts

HAYLEY: There're reasons

GREG: Personal reasons

HAYLEY: Medical reasons

GREG: Sorry, medical reasons

HAYLEY: You've seen how my hands are

GREG: No proof, have you

HAYLEY: Not that kind of

GREG: My son, he got better soon as I threatened to take his X-Box away

HAYLEY: Now you're just confusing the

GREG: At the end of the day in this day and age you don't have to stop to pull out of a project because of some little thing like your hands don't work

I know a chap steadily losing another ten per cent of his eyesight year on year, can't see a bloody thing now, 'cept blobs and colours and he's working at board level, bright as a button. Someone to do his reading for him, help him up and down stairs but otherwise

So I don't see why you can't get your team of silly haircutted little buggers to do the lifting and carrying for you and let you get on with the thinking bit of the job, the ideas and

HAYLEY: I'm not sure if you realise how debilitating

GREG: I'm sure to you it feels like the whole bloody world's falling apart because you can't pick up your chopsticks, change gear on that natty little car

HAYLEY: It's an automatic

GREG: Still driving?

HAYLEY: Well no, can't grip the wheel

GREG: Looks like the sky is falling down then, doesn't it?

Beat.

If my son got better, pulled himself together or forgot about it or

HAYLEY: Did he go to the doctors?

GREG: Well yes but

HAYLEY: What did they give him?

GREG: Injections

HAYLEY: So he didn't just pull himself together I mean he needed something

GREG: You could get injections

HAYLEY: No

GREG: Why not?

HAYLEY: I

Needles. Don't like them

GREG: How's that going down with the boss?

HAYLEY: I do have the support of the partners they've

GREG: This must affect your prospects, though, mustn't it?

HAYLEY: Please

GREG: As groovy as they try to be, as inclusive and liberal

Not really going to want a partner with gammy hands are they?

Not very groovy, not very slick

When you could do something but you won't and you're too ill to do your hair neatly

HAYLEY touches her hair.

Sorry, too personal?

HAYLEY: They don't

GREG: Did it get too personal?

Do they know how personal it got?

Beat.

HAYLEY: Knowing how personal it got, won't it be easier not to have me around?

GREG: I don't know

Woke me up, you did. Almost got me back to the land of the living, bit of an overhaul. Human Performance Review

Brought me out of deep freeze

Sorry if I'm a bit bitter you couldn't

See it through

HAYLEY: I'm sorry, / I didn't

GREG: Are we done?

HAYLEY looks at GREG, then at her lap.

HAYLEY: I need

I need you to sign something

GREG: Do you?

HAYLEY: To say that you're

That you understand the changes to the team working on the project, that I won't be heading it up anymore

GREG: What if I don't sign it?

HAYLEY: There's no reason not to sign it

GREG: Would it piss you off?

HAYLEY: That's not

GREG: No, too personal

Beat.

Have a look at it then

HAYLEY: OK

HAYLEY very painstakingly picks up her bag from the floor and tries to slide a piece of paper out of it. GREG watches her. She manages to get the paper out, but it slips from her fingers and floats to the floor.

Just a second

GREG sits back in his chair. HAYLEY bends down and tries to scoop up the piece of paper with both hands. Eventually she gets a grip on it and places it on her side of the desk. GREG looks at her.

GREG: You'll have to pass it to me.

HAYLEY looks at him. She makes a decision.

HAYLEY: Fucker

She bends down to the table and picks up the piece of paper between her teeth. She walks around to GREG's side of the table and places it in front of him, then stands waiting for him to sign.

I trust you've got a pen.

GREG: Yes

GREG takes a pen from his suit pocket and signs the piece of paper. He looks at HAYLEY standing over him.

There. Done.

He stands up, picks up the paper and walks around to HAYLEY's side of the desk. He replaces the paper carefully in her laptop bag and then opens the door for her to leave.

HAYLEY: OK

HAYLEY walks towards her bag to pick it up.

OK

GREG takes the bag and gently places it on HAYLEY's shoulder for her. She tries to smile at him.

Thanks.

I'd shake your hand but

GREG: Yeah.

HAYLEY leaves. GREG sits back down. He looks at the sunflowers. He touches the petals of one of them, gently. He leans in to sniff the flowers, to see if they have a smell. They don't. He sits back in his chair and looks at them. — you can see them but you can't touch them

Fade.

Scene 12

HAYLEY and STEVE's flat. Early evening. The place is a mess.

STEVE comes in and sniffs the air. He frowns. He goes to the kitchen counter. He opens a cupboard with a strap and takes out a package – it's a batch of cortisone injections. He tries to open the packet with his hands but fails. Frustrated, he tries to open it with his teeth, but that doesn't work either. He hears movement outside the room, and quickly hides the packet.

HAYLEY comes through the door. She is wearing STEVE's pyjamas. They look at each other.

HAYLEY: Borrowed your jamas, sorry

STEVE: OK.

HAYLEY looks away. She goes to sit on the sofa, facing away from STEVE.

STEVE looks at her, goes to say something, but doesn't. He looks at the space beside the bread-bin, then sighs. He slides the lid of the bread-bin up with his forearm and takes out a wrapped loaf of bread. He picks it up with both forearms and shakes two slices out onto the counter. He picks them up with flat hands and puts them into the toaster. He uses his forearm to push the lever of the toaster down.

As he is doing this HAYLEY turns and goes to say something, but doesn't. She lies down on the sofa, awkwardly pulls a blanket over her and closes her eyes to sleep.

STEVE looks over to the sofa and sees HAYLEY lying down. He takes a few steps towards her. He watches her sleep for a few moments, then presses the cancel button on the toaster. The bread pops up again, untoasted. Disfunctional / Cancel the relationship

STEVE leaves the room. The heat is gone

Fade.

Scene 13

GREG's office. Afternoon.

There is now a new bunch of Interflora flowers on GREG's desk – not sunflowers this time, but something more romantic. LYDIA stands on GREG's side of the desk, changing the printer cartridge of GREG's printer. GREG stands beside her, a stop-watch in his hand.

LYDIA: Nearly there.

> *LYDIA closes the lid of the printer and sits in GREG's chair. She looks at the screen and clicks the mouse. The printer churns out a page. LYDIA hands it to GREG.*

> Test page.

> *GREG stops the stop-watch.*

GREG: Good

> *LYDIA smiles. She gets up out of his chair.*

> Pretty good

LYDIA: Bit more difficult with someone timing you

GREG: You didn't panic

> *GREG indicates for LYDIA to sit down opposite him.*

> Please

LYDIA: Thank you.

> *GREG looks at LYDIA's CV.*

> Nice flowers

GREG: Secret admirer

LYDIA: Lovely

GREG: They're all going mad out there trying to work out who sent them

LYDIA: Office gossip

> Your wife or

GREG: Doubt it

> *GREG looks down at the CV again.*

> So. Good with computers

LYDIA: Pretty good

GREG: I'm hopeless

Need all the help I can get

LYDIA: I think everyone

Everyone finds it scary

GREG: Yes

LYDIA: Or most people

GREG: Yes

LYDIA: Apart from, you know, actual computer people

GREG: Yes

LYDIA: And even they sometimes don't

GREG: No

LYDIA: And you wonder really, don't you, about taking advice from guys who wear Velcro shoes to work?

GREG laughs.

GREG: Yes

LYDIA: Because you think they can solve everything for you but actually

Beat.

GREG: And other things, what about other things

LYDIA: I'll do anything, I'll make tea

GREG: You wouldn't be opposed

LYDIA: To making tea?

GREG: For a colleague

LYDIA: No, I wouldn't I'd quite like it

To see that someone needed a cup of tea and to make it for them, to identify that need

I mean that's human interaction, isn't it?

GREG: Yes

LYDIA: Just kindness. I do think people should be kinder to people I mean

Not a very trendy thing to say is it, these days

But I'd much rather have a cup of tea made for me by a *person* with a kettle and a tea-bag than just the drinks machine, you know?

Someone who'd noticed I needed one

Beat.

This is a new role, is it?

GREG: Had some consultants in, expecting they'd demand I cull a secretary or two

Not actually *cull*, you know, but

LYDIA: Yes

GREG: Turns out I need *more* people, they reckon a competent Office Manager's just the thing to smooth out the, sorry *optimise efficiency*

Do you say 'schedule' or 'schedule'?

LYDIA: Um, 'schedule's the English one, isn't it?

GREG: And you say that

LYDIA: Yes

Yes

Or sometimes just 'diary'

GREG: Diary. Like it

Anything you'd like to ask?

LYDIA: Um when will you

GREG: Tomorrow, probably

LYDIA: Well, my number's on my CV so if you need anything else, need to know anything else

LYDIA stands up, shakes GREG's hand confidently and goes to the door. She touches the door handle then turns back.

Um

GREG: Yes?

LYDIA: You should probably know that

Because they'll probably tell you when you call up for references

There was um

It wasn't just overstaffing that got me the redundancy, there was an incident as well

Unfortunately

And you should probably know because it did have some / impact

GREG: I know about the incident, I called them yesterday

You held a door open

LYDIA: Trying to identify a need, I

GREG: Everyone makes mistakes

LYDIA: Yes

GREG: The good people learn

LYDIA: I learned

 I really did learn

 Thank you.

 GREG smiles. LYDIA smiles.

 Fade.

Scene 14

HAYLEY and STEVE's flat. Early evening.

HAYLEY is asleep on the sofa wearing STEVE's pyjamas, her hands folded across her chest like a mummy. STEVE comes in wearing boxer shorts and carrying an empty bin-bag under his arm. He goes to a pile of clothes on the floor and shakes his feet into a pair of jogging pants, then attempts to pull them up using flat hands. HAYLEY wakes up, blinks, looks at STEVE. He sees HAYLEY watching him.

STEVE: Who needs buttons, huh?

 HAYLEY smiles.

HAYLEY: Hm

STEVE: You sleep?

HAYLEY: Yeah

 STEVE carefully pulls on a T-shirt, again keeping his hands flat, his fingers together. HAYLEY laughs.

STEVE: What?

HAYLEY: Look like a penguin or something

STEVE: Yeah.

 STEVE tries to open the bin-bag by blowing on its edge. HAYLEY looks at him.

 Thought I'd tidy up a bit

 Lydia's coming round

HAYLEY: Is she?

STEVE: Cooking us dinner

HAYLEY: Right

STEVE: Wants to help me look after you

Beat.

Might want to put some clothes on

HAYLEY: Yeah

STEVE: Doesn't matter if you

HAYLEY: No, I will

Look like a

STEVE: She doesn't mind

HAYLEY: Look like a jumble sale

STEVE: You look lovely

HAYLEY: Steve

STEVE: What?

HAYLEY: Don't be sweet I'll cry

STEVE: You alright?

HAYLEY: Want to get better

STEVE: Takes time

HAYLEY: Yeah

STEVE: Think mine might be on the mend

Bit better

HAYLEY: Really?

STEVE: Those injections

HAYLEY looks away.

Sorry

HAYLEY: What's dinner?

STEVE: She said maybe stir-fry

HAYLEY looks away.

Oh

HAYLEY: What?

STEVE: Cutlery

HAYLEY: Oh

STEVE: We'll think of something

HAYLEY: Yeah

HAYLEY stands up.

Brush my hair

She looks for her hairbrush.

Where've I put my

It's on the kitchen counter.

Look

Living like a tramp

STEVE has got the bag open and starts to pick up debris from the floor – tissues, food-packaging. HAYLEY picks up the hairbrush and carries it back to the sofa.

STEVE: Not forever, is it?

HAYLEY starts to brush her hair slowly. The movement hurts. STEVE watches. She gets to a knot in her hair which she can't get the brush through. She gives up and throws the brush across the room.

HAYLEY: Fucker.

STEVE: Hey

HAYLEY: Ow

HAYLEY cradles her hand.

STEVE: Hayley

HAYLEY: I just

I can't

STEVE goes to pick up the brush. He looks at her.

I think we're

I can't *do* anything I can't even

STEVE: You started it you did start it

HAYLEY looks at him.

You said you wanted to sleep with someone else

HAYLEY looks away.

HAYLEY: I said I wanted to it didn't mean I would

Didn't mean I was going to

STEVE: Why not?

HAYLEY: Because I didn't really want to, I just wanted you to *mind*.

Beat.

STEVE: I did mind

HAYLEY: You didn't say you minded, you didn't show it or

STEVE hands the brush back to HAYLEY. She looks at him for a long time.

D'you think we can fix this?

Pause. The question hangs in the air.

The doorbell rings.

STEVE: That'll be

HAYLEY: Steve

STEVE: Lydia's here I'll

STEVE goes to answer the door. HAYLEY looks at her hands. LYDIA comes into the room carrying shopping-bags, followed by STEVE. She's wearing smart office clothes.

LYDIA: No I thought of the cutlery problem too but then I was in the Chinese supermarket and they had these

Hi Hayley

HAYLEY: Hi

LYDIA pulls a packet of extra-wide straws out of a shopping-bag.

LYDIA: Look, big straws

Apparently there's some mad Chinese drink with bits in

HAYLEY: Bubble tea

LYDIA: So I thought these'd be perfect so as long I cut things up small you'll be able to suck it up, you'll be able to feed yourselves solid food

Might look a bit silly but

STEVE: No, great

Hayley

HAYLEY: Thank you

LAURA WADE

> *LYDIA unpacks the shopping. HAYLEY watches her inhabit the kitchen.*

> *Silence. STEVE looks at HAYLEY.*

LYDIA: So anyway the job's fine

STEVE: Sorry. Yeah. Job

LYDIA: Started this morning

STEVE: And?

LYDIA: Great. Knackered

Nice people

HAYLEY: You got a job

LYDIA: Just a boring office job, nothing special. No big deal

> *LYDIA finishes the unpacking. She puts the empty plastic bags in the bin and looks up to see STEVE and HAYLEY both watching her.*

(*To STEVE.*) Dinner'll take like twenty minutes did you want to do the thing first?

STEVE: Yeah

LYDIA: You got them

STEVE: Here

LYDIA: OK

> *STEVE takes a package from the kitchen and sits on the sofa. HAYLEY moves away.*

HAYLEY: Oh god I'm shutting my eyes

> *LYDIA goes to sit by STEVE on the sofa. During this she opens the package and takes out a syringe.*

STEVE: So you like it, you like the people?

LYDIA: New boss took me for a drink this evening, funny chap

> *HAYLEY stands nervously by the kitchen, her arms around herself. LYDIA holds the syringe in her hand, gesturing as she talks.*

Keeps getting all these flowers delivered to him, and he's a proper bloke, married and everything so the whole office is trying to work out who they're from and either he doesn't know or he's not telling, whole place in a constant state of expectation you can feel it fizzing

Anyway we go for this drink, just me and him and

He tells me just out of the blue he's sent them to himself – like the first bunch was from someone, he wouldn't tell me who, but he liked it so he's been sending them himself, a bunch a week, pretending it's

And now they all think he's fantastic and he's got this new smile because of it so

LYDIA injects STEVE.

And I'm suddenly this person people tell things to I can't imagine why he told me but it makes me

Yeah

LYDIA removes the needle.

Done.

STEVE rubs his hand. He looks at LYDIA. He stands up.

Other one?

STEVE: Hayley

HAYLEY: Yeah

STEVE: There's another shot

HAYLEY shakes her head.

HAYLEY: I can't

Silence.

STEVE and HAYLEY look at each other. STEVE flexes his fingers.

STEVE: Really helps, you know

Once it stops hurting you can actually *think*

LYDIA: Hayley?

HAYLEY: It's needles you know I

STEVE: I'll hold you

I just think we've got to be braver.

HAYLEY comes slowly to the sofa and sits between STEVE's legs. He puts his arms around her waist. LYDIA prepares the shot. HAYLEY screws her face up.

HAYLEY: Aah

STEVE: Brave

HAYLEY: Yeah

HAYLEY holds her hand out for LYDIA to inject and buries her head in STEVE's shoulder. LYDIA injects HAYLEY's hand.

Tss. Ow.

LYDIA: Nearly done

Nearly done

It'll be better before you know it.

Fade.

The end.